when
my
ghost
sings

when my

ghost

TARA SIDHOO FRASER

A Memoir of
Stroke, Recovery &
Transformation

ARSENAL PULP PRESS
VANCOUVER

ARSENAL PULP PRESS
Suite 202 – 211 East Georgia St.
Vancouver, BC V6A 1Z6
Canada
arsenalpulp.com

The publisher gratefully acknowledges the support of the Canada Council for the Arts
and the British Columbia Arts Council for its publishing program, and the Government of
Canada and the Government of British Columbia (through the Book Publishing Tax Credit
Program) for its publishing activities.

Arsenal Pulp Press acknowledges the xʷməθkʷəy̓əm (Musqueam), Sḵwx̱wú7mesh
(Squamish), and səlilwətaɫ (Tsleil-Waututh) Nations, custodians of the traditional, ancestral,
and unceded territories where our office is located. We pay respect to their histories,
traditions, and continuous living cultures and commit to accountability, respectful relations,
and friendship.

Cover and text design by Jazmin Welch
Cover art by Christine Kim, *Celadon*, 2022, 23.25″ × 16.25″ x 2.25″, mixed media diorama
in pencil, watercolours, and charcoal on cotton rag paper
Edited by Catharine Chen
Proofread by Alison Strobel

Printed and bound in Canada

Library and Archives Canada Cataloguing in Publication:
Title: When my ghost sings : a memoir of stroke, recovery & transformation /
   Tara Sidhoo Fraser.
Names: Fraser, Tara Sidhoo, author.
Identifiers: Canadiana (print) 20230210716 | Canadiana (ebook) 20230210740 |
   ISBN 9781551529271 (softcover) | ISBN 9781551529288 (EPUB)
Subjects: LCSH: Fraser, Tara Sidhoo—Health. | LCSH: Amnesiacs—Canada—Biography. |
   LCSH: Cerebrovascular disease—Patients—Canada—Biography. | LCGFT: Autobiographies.
Classification: LCC RC394.A5 F73 2023 | DDC 616.85/2320092—dc23

For Ghost and the boy

CONTENTS

On that day in November of 2014, I was thirty-two years old when the blood vessels that connect my left thalamus to my brain stem ballooned and burst, resulting in a slow bleed. My stroke was due to a rare mutation called an arteriovenous malformation (AVM). AVMS are relatively rare cerebral lesions that occur at or before birth, and over time, their risk of bursting increases. Unfortunately, AVMS are usually asymptomatic until a brain bleed occurs.

The brain is filled with vessels and capillaries. I've been told to picture them like roadways and streets, to imagine my blood as a vehicle. In a regularly functioning brain, all of the vessels slow down the blood and ensure that nutrients and oxygen are properly dispersed throughout the body. But my brain is different. Due to the AVM, my vessels are tangled and missing capillaries, so my blood races from my arteries to my veins until it bursts through the walls of my vessels.

An AVM is assessed for how risky open neurological surgery would be by size, location, and complexity of venous drainage. Because my AVM is large, stretching from my left thalamus all the way down to my brain stem, it has been deemed inoperable. So, instead of surgery, an embolization was performed to stop the flow of blood through my tangled vessels.

Today, while the majority of my AVM has been embolized, there is still a small, sensitive section deep in my brain stem that was left alone, a section that the doctors did not feel it was safe to embolize.

CHAPTER 1

The Memory Box

YOU LOVED THE SUMMER. I know this because I still have all of your photographs. In this one, you are sprawled over concrete, tanning yourself beneath the suburban sun. This picture was captured by someone who loved you; this I know because you are smiling and your eyes are warm. Behind you is the back of a white stuccoed house, a weeping willow to one side of it. You tell me that this is where Mama hangs the family's underwear on the laundry line for everyone to see, and it kills you with embarrassment. Thick stalks of grass grow under the line, overlooking the garden bed. Mama's garden has raspberry bushes and rich soil. It must be late afternoon in the photo because the heat is thick, your body damp. You are surrounded by ancient dandelions and the wild grass tickles your thighs as you longingly gaze through the widened slits of the wooden fence toward the back laneway. The other side.

My memory, your memory, says that there is neither an end nor a beginning to this street. That there is nothing beyond the white stuccoed home and Mama's garden patch. That there is only the grass and the raspberry bushes. Even though, according to maps and to other stories, we are both aware that Charland Avenue is a dead-end street. So, there is an ending. There is a beginning.

It is quiet here. When the sun disappears and the night blankets everything, I can hear faint footsteps in the upstairs kitchen and someone washing dishes. I can remember squeezing my eyes shut to capture shapes of orange and black. And that a gang of children has claimed the woods by the house as their territory.

In the laneway behind the house on Charland Avenue, the neighbourhood children's stained sneakers hover over the pebbled concrete. Against the pale sky lies a ravine with dampened leaves and muddied waters. This is where the children played. This is where you played. The trees serve as forts for the young and backrests for mopey teenagers swimming in oversized hoodies, necks decorated with thick chains and metal spikes. Their frail bodies slumped against the wide tree trunks. Your friends. Your memories.

See, here you are during puberty, that difficult transition from goblin to elder goblin. Another picture of you drinking in the heat. Eyes caked in thick liner, lips dressed in fuchsia. The dark lipstick reminds me of women with voices enriched by whiskey and cigarettes—their crackled chorus melts my heart.

Remember this.

Low-waisted shorts grip your hip bones, while your arms, still a blank canvas, reach upward, toward the sky. You look as though you are praying to the heat. Summer is my season as well. We share this. My skin also drinks the light, breathes a sigh of relief after enduring the long winter months. I pray to the sun, thank her for warming my body.

Nestled in the photo album, there is a cola-stained Polaroid of an amusement park. Your hand gripping the thin string of a balloon, your freshly shaven head resting on a pale boy's shoulder. These days, he lives in a crooked farmhouse down a thin road in Mount Finlayson where, at night, when there are no lights, the stars swallow the lane-way and blur your vision. You only have one photograph of the boy, but he says you were close. Thick as thieves.

This photo album lives in Ghost's memory box, nestled among her ratty T-shirts and hardcover journals whose pages are filled with words that wash over the outer edges of the paper. There is only one entry from the day Ghost disappeared. A few shaky letters squeezed together, their bodies gasping for air. These letters, from that day in November, are her last song.

When I ask Ghost what she wants, she grasps my heart, licks her lips, and whispers stories. She narrates her life in faded photographs and silent films that are buried in various areas of my body. In the marrow of my femur, she stores the subway's sticky seats, charcoal-covered fingers, a nude self-portrait that burned her cheeks when displayed on the wall next to everyone else's fully clothed renditions of themselves. And Meredith. There is a thinly veiled memory of Meredith that Ghost has carved into my right thumbnail. Beneath certain light I can see it ingrained in the deep grooves that run vertically across the nail bed.

Meredith.

Whenever I slip the tip of my index finger over the grooves, Ghost smacks her lips and begins.

Dent number one: Meredith's mouth is a thin wire stretching from one cheek to the other.

Dent number two: Sisters is the nightclub where the music rico-chets through Ghost's bones, where she meets Meredith in the dark.

Neon lights skitter across the floor, and Meredith's hair shimmers. There is a red door in the corner of the club, and someone is knocking.

Dent number three: Meredith and Ghost are in the back alley. From somewhere far away, the low murmur of cars buzzes over the metal trash bins, past concrete houses and unlit street lights. This is when Ghost's heart explodes for the first time beneath the faded moon, her breath stained with sweet soda water and gin.

And every other kiss I did not understand until today ... Ghost's love note to Meredith, journal number five.

Dent number four: Ghost plays this film for me in small flashes while squeezing my esophagus with her tiny hands until my breath stops and everything is silent. There is a futon, with soft petals decorating the bedspread. Ghost is curled beneath the blankets, lips glistening with saliva, quivering, holding the weight of the news.

This all happened well before she moved to an island in the middle of the sea. Years before she met the boy.

But the boy who lives in the crooked farmhouse says he knows a different tale. When I describe the postcards that accompany my nail dents, he shakes his head and fills in the missing pieces.

"Not like that," he corrects me. "Meredith was brief. You only had two dates, remember?"

And then Ghost whines as the boy finds her missteps; her postcard images shudder and transform into the boy's tale.

Meredith, with her shaggy hair and distant eyes, swims from the bedroom to the bathroom, and it is time to leave. Ghost confesses to Meredith that her heart is singing. Meredith's eyes are distant as she sips her coffee and explains that she is leaving for New York in a few weeks, where another woman is waiting for her. Ghost's cheeks burn the same colour they did in class because she is naked all over again, and the audience—Meredith—is fully clothed.

On the palm of my hand are deep curved lines that split like tender stalks of grass. These are Ghost's lifelines, built with inconsistent memories.

The memory box helps. Her old photographs serve as evidence, helping to prove or disprove a story, showing me what is and what was. Tangible evidence. I can't rely only on Ghost's mental postcards because she is a liar who forgets the truth and magnifies her desires.

Ghost has only a few photographs from the old days. One is of the beach house. This was while her mama and John were still married. After John left, the family photographs stopped, and then Ghost left, and the world was undocumented for many years.

Ghost tells me that the beach house is tan, and the paint is fresh. There are white tiles in the kitchen, and the living room floor is built from the darkest wood of the tree's trunk. There is a bookshelf with romance novels—on their covers, blond men whose muscles tear through their ruffled blouses—and a long window that looks out on the lake. Ghost tells me this is where she'd sit for hours, listening to the water's waves.

In the photograph, the beach is cool. I know because, even though the sun is shining, Ghost is dressed in an oversized white T-shirt and a long, heavy skirt. Her hair is tangled with the lake's breath as it grazes the land. Resting beside her is a yellow raft with rubbery paddles. Ghost has slipped the seaside story into my left molar, somewhere just above the tooth's roots and below its silver crown.

She tells me that this photograph was captured just after she'd ventured out in a storm, beneath leggy flashes of lightning. She says that her inflatable raft tossed about in the dark water as she tumbled into the murky horizon, farther and farther from the shoreline.

"One Mississippi, two Mississippi, three Mississippi ..." the photographed little Ghost bellows into the sky, until the lightning fades.

But when I tell Mama about the lakeside storm, she shakes her head. Mama says that it began as a light afternoon drizzle, and Ghost was very close to the shoreline. After the rain thickened into fat droplets, Mama called for Ghost to come inside for lunch. She and Ghost watched the rainfall from the kitchen window over a warm bowl of tomato soup.

I wince when Mama shares the part about tomato soup. After that day in November, I spent months sucking broth off heavy spoons, trying to lick up what spilled down my chin. Afterward came pills and then sleep, until I would wake up and do it all over again. Ghost hates this thought; she seethes and kicks my throat until I am gasping for words. That day is rarely discussed; it has been slipped under another one of my muscles, somewhere far away. Other people have their own stories of the days that followed but thankfully, they all agree with Ghost's version of that November morning, so I know it is honest. Sometimes, she will alter the landscape until the crystal sky melts into a rosy hue, or play with the trees until they darken and steam, but the most important threads of the tale never change. To Ghost, the story of that November morning is important because it tells me how she died.

CHAPTER 2

The Graduation Certificate

I LIVE IN AN APARTMENT WITH DUSTY MICE who gnaw the edge of the wall beams, while outside, seagulls sing in the early morning hours. Before the sun swells with life, while the air is still a hazy grey, the creamy birds gather one by one until they fill my balcony. Their floppy feet trip across the metal banister as they dance, stretching their beaks to call the morning light. Even the mice pause from their job of tunnel building to listen to the seagulls' ballad.

I drag my body from the button-studded futon and stumble into the kitchenette, which is also part of the bedroom and the living room. There is a little silver coffee maker big enough to brew just two cups of coffee, or one Thermos full. Next to the coffee maker is my graduation certificate. Encased in glass, it sits on my kitchen counter beneath a collection of bills and half-filled notebooks. I am still unsure where I should put it. Mama says I should hang it in my living room for all to see. She is convinced that this graduation is a stepping stone, even though we are both unsure what it is a stepping stone to.

When Mama talks about my graduation, she does so with pride. Her lips stretch across her face and she dips her chin up and down as she tells her audience about the complications and my perseverance.

"You have accomplished so much. You should be proud." Her oceanic voice swims over my sternum, filling me with shame. Ghost is riddled with guilt as well when she listens to Mama's pride, as we are both aware that I barely graduated and had to drop my minor.

I want to tell Mama that my graduation is not a celebratory matter. That I was not, in fact, a "good student," driven to articulate my thoughts and expand my mind. If I had been, this would be an entirely different story.

Instead of spending nights at the library, wrapped up in books, I spent my time with a woman named Sam whose lips were always stained with gin. Beneath dim halos of light, we would sit at the bar on thick wooden stools, sipping dizzy drinks that painted our lashes with desire.

As the music groaned through the speakers, Sam would press her lips together before finishing each one of her drinks.

"Are you ready?" she would ask, her handsome face decorated with deep lines that defined her eyes. And I would smile, take one more sip before slipping my hand on her knee because she enjoyed my public affection. She said she enjoyed showing me off.

This all took place during a sullen winter, barely a year after that day in November. The roads were grey beneath the faded street lamps. It was February. The last time I saw Sam, we stood near the docks, her heavy cologne tickling my throat, which was already sour from a few drinks at the pub, and I watched her eyes narrow and grow distant as we traded farewells.

So, Mama, you are mistaken.

My time in the university library was spent wandering the aisles aimlessly, pausing to pull books off the shelves—not to read them, but only to appreciate their covers. Their cracked casings of faded fabric marked with dents. Their pages yellowed by the laborious hands of other students.

When I did read articles, I did not get far. Ghost would cast her eyes over my own until the letters jumbled and sentences danced all across the page. Until I could no longer follow the story. Each sentence jumped until I grew dizzy attempting to swallow the information and grasp the point.

By then Ghost would grow bored and begin clawing at my esophagus and pushing her legs against my rib cage until my stomach stretched and rounded, until the button clasping my pants closed threatened to burst. And I would throw my hands over my face and push them against my eyes until the world was dark and I was swallowed by it.

By this point, Ghost would wrap her body with every one of my vessels and beg for me to call Sam again, because being dizzy with Sam felt safer than being dizzy alone.

These were small acts of torture: the bloated belly, Ghost's buried desires. I would cram my papers in my backpack and bolt from the student library and make my way to the bus stop. On the way there, I would dial Sam's number. She always picked up; she always knew when I needed her.

"Hello, sweetheart." Her voice drawled through the receiver before settling down comfortably. "Yes, yes, I'm always available to see you. Of course I'll buy your ticket. I miss you too."

And I would quickly run home and bundle clean underwear, a toothbrush, and makeup into my knapsack. And my breath would catch because now, Ghost was grabbing my heart and skipping it over my breastbone and down my back until it was dancing faster than the sentences in the books. And this let me know that she was pleased with my decision because visiting with Sam was much nicer than wasting time at the library.

It would already be dark by the time the ferry reached Seattle. In February, the sun fades early, and the streets, cloaked with icy rain, shimmer beneath the street lamps. Even if Sam had already had a few drinks, she'd promise that she was able to drive. She'd say her body was stronger than most and that the alcohol no longer affected her vision. Sam's small white Honda slowly bumbled across the city and into a small suburb that sounded like someone's name. She said that she preferred manuals because they were more cost efficient and easier to control.

Each time I pressed my lips against hers, I tasted the salty reminder of her last drink, and she'd pause, pull back. She struggled with guilt. Her dark eyes sank into shame, her pupils edged with worry.

"I'm too old for you," she'd mutter.

And in response, I'd run my fingers through her short hair and sigh as Ghost clutched my voice box and whispered rebuttals into her ear.

"No, you're not. I like you. This is fun."

And then Sam would lean into me, and after a while her fingers found my zipper, and this was better than falling into the dancing words, this was easier than that.

Sam didn't see the point of bed frames; she thought they were bulky and difficult to move. She told me that constantly moving was second nature to her, that if she stayed stagnant for too long the world faded, became subdued. Her mattress was comfortable though, thick and padded, wrapped in cotton sheets, and topped with a feather duvet that she'd cocoon around me before lulling me to sleep with stories from her days working at some medical factory in Ohio, where she was from. She told me that one day, once she was finished with Seattle, she would move back there.

"Tell me about the tiny towns with gazebos," I would say, taking her hand and placing it on my breast. In these moments, Ghost would lie still, intoxicated by warmth and lust. I'd rest my head on Sam's chest and match her breathing, try to connect through her inhale and exhale, allow the night to blanket me in its own hypnotic breath.

"And in the factory," Sam's voice traced through the dark, "there was this little prick who was the same level as me but acted like he had all this authority ..."

"Mm-hmm."

"Ned the prick, that's what we all called him, 'cause he didn't know up from down. He always had his snout in the air, like a little mouse. Probably because he was younger and trying to prove himself. One day, he just strolls up to me with his mousy face and accuses me of taking too long on my breaks. So, you know what I did? I flipped him the bird, 'cause what he didn't know but the actual managers did was that my breaks were all combined ..."

"Ned's a prick," I would agree, feeling Sam's body soften and invite me to nuzzle deeper into her chest.

So, Mama, you are mistaken.

My final two semesters of school were not notable. I was not a fresh-faced student, lapping up information, my mind busily connecting theories; I let Ghost take over. On the days that I did try, when I was tiptoeing onward responsibly and completing my assignments, I had to work on the third floor of the library, which was known as the silent floor. High above the other floors, it was a separate layer of the building, void of chaos. Below the third floor, it was all swift movements and chatter, lively students who moved too quickly; they drove my Ghost into fits of anger. I'd feel her fists slamming into my teeth, and I would clench my jaw and walk briskly past the busy aisles, scuttle up the stairs to our safe haven.

With the chaos of the floors below contained, the third floor was calm. There, I would settle into one of the cubicles, surrounded by hazy walls and fluorescent lights, and be able to stare at the busy letters on the paper and taste-test bits of information from lengthy articles printed in small fonts. Ghost and I quietly trained our brain to connect the dots.

But, Mama, I was unable to remember most of what I read. After a while, the lines were meaningless. They did not make sense. They collapsed on one another like dominoes. And so I wrote papers crammed with full-bodied citations that did not connect or have any linear logic. So many citations that there were no original concepts in any of the work I handed in. Ghost whined that these assignments were dull and pounded her bony fists against my temples, demanding that I call Sam for drinks and softness.

Now, the piece of paper that titles me as educated is trapped in glass, hidden beneath bills and junk mail, and now, it is almost spring, and I haven't spoken to Sam in quite a while. It is early, so it is still dark. I know that outside there are trees stretching from the seaside soil into the dampened air. I know that these trees are beginning to sprout bits of yellow now that they have finally finished baring their bodies to the winter. I know that the pavement is damp and the air is still icy, still frozen.

CHAPTER 3

Ghost the Dancer

MAMA TELLS ME THAT GHOST WAS A DANCER. She shows me photographs she has saved in her own memory box, which also holds pearls, ruby earrings, and golden bangles from her own mama. In India, jewellery is generational, passed down and then down and then down again, from one daughter to the next, and so on. Mama says that one day, I will wear her amethyst necklace. When she reminds me of this, Ghost shifts with discomfort and her long fingers crawl up my neck and clasp my tongue so that I cannot speak. She does this because we both understand that Mama's jewels are not meant for me; they are meant for Ghost.

Mama has ancient tales, heated by memories of afternoon sun in the big backyard that at one time was an orchard. Each story is painted with softness because, back then, John and Mama were still in love. But as Mama's voice swims over my ears, decorating the landscape with low storefronts and quiet neighbourhoods, Ghost fidgets and squeezes my shoulders until my body slouches forward and my back rounds, because we both understand that Mama's memories do not include us.

On Charland Avenue, Ghost was a dancer. Mama has photographs of her daughter wearing tutus and shiny hair decorations at dance recitals, paper programs from school shows, and a video cassette titled "Cinderella in Tights" that was filmed by John. Mama asks to watch the video sometimes, hoping that we can both remember those days. That was during her time on Charland Avenue, when Ghost and John were both still around. So, we sit, watching the grainy little dancers on the television. But Ghost has not saved these memories; she has her own films.

Ghost's films of dance are lodged in my Achilles heel, beneath the thickened vessels, somewhere deep within my muscle tissue, so that Ghost does not need Mama's memories to tell the story.

Her room is wallpapered with simple squares, a cream-coloured pattern on a beige background. Ghost sits cross-legged, decorated with plastic treasures strewn around her neck. She splays her fingers between plump plastic emeralds and candy-like rubies, wrapping her body in her riches. These treasures follow her everywhere. Down the beige-carpeted hallway, into the kitchen, she slams through the swinging door, her jewels glittering.

And now, she is in her bedroom. As she pulls on thick white tights that squeeze her belly and leave marks on her skin, the necklaces sway. As she shimmies a tight black leotard up over her thighs, over her chest, her treasures bunch and gleam in the sunlight until this film fades, until the pictures are floating like birds over my muscles, still protected by my skin. Somewhere in the dark, Ghost finds my hand and guides me past the filmy grey roads back to her house on Charland Avenue. We climb into Mama's dark-green gremlin of a car with explosions of red rust over the doors and float toward the dance hall. Sometimes John drives. He likes to speed; when John drives, the houses fly by as if you are on a fairground ride. Ghost enjoys this. She feels special in the fast car with the windows down and the wind tangling her hair.

And now, and now, I can see her rose-coloured slippers and thick white tights. Mama is seated in a plastic chair, and the dance instructor, who has a long torso and wears a blueberry-coloured cardigan, is smiling, and now everyone is laughing over the piano's tune. The one-room dance studio has mirrored walls and stained tiles with dark scuff marks.

Mama has a photo of this too.

The dance centre is on a busy street, with fast cars and chirping crosswalks, but there is a quieter area behind the building, where the parents park. This is where Ghost and I sit on a concrete parking stop outside the studio and warm our backs in the sun. Across the way, there is a giant oak tree surrounded by yellowed grass next to a lonely swing set. The tree's grotesque roots suffocate the grass. The thick heat wraps itself around our bodies until we are damp, and everything begins to blur and fade. And the ancient dandelions smear into nothingness.

CHAPTER 4

Jude

IT IS MID-MARCH when the internet introduces Jude and I to one another. Jude is bright. I like their profile photos. There are pictures of the sun across the water, of courtyard parties, road adventures, of their serious mouth and iridescent eyes. At first glance they are a smoky quartz, a murky blend of hazel and grey, but in certain light you can make out thin waves of blue, gashes of plum. During our first conversation, Jude tells me that their eyes reveal their mood.

I live on Vancouver Island, across from the mainland of BC, and Jude is a fresh face in the coastal city of Seattle, a recent transplant from San Francisco. They say that figuratively burrowing their feet into the cold Seattle soil is taking much longer than expected. That lacking a community of friendly queers is a terrible reminder of what they used to have.

I nod to myself, slipping my fingers between the beige tufts of my carpet, the telephone nuzzled between my shoulder and my ear as Jude laments living in a new city with no friends.

"Yes, it is difficult. I don't have a community either," I agreed. "Living on this island feels lonely."

"Are people friendly there?" they ask.

"Yes, friendly, just quiet and different ... from me."

It isn't that Victoria is devoid of queers. Just the opposite. There are queer people and events everywhere. I just do not feel connected to them. As I said, I am different.

"I realized how different Seattle is just a few months after arriving. I miss how easy it was to meet other queers in San Francisco. How does everyone here meet people?"

"I'm not sure. The internet?"

Jude and I speak on the telephone for a few hours every night. Long after the sky is dark, I lie on my stained carpet and stare up at the frosted ceiling, allowing Jude's stories to tug at my eardrum and tickle my heart. I like Jude. I like their deep cello voice and their stories.

"Tell me more about when you were at sea in Italy," I ask Jude.

Outside it's raining again. Small pocks dot the ceiling. Water stains. Large tan circles surround the spots.

"The days are humid and drag out. And at night the stars are so clear. I still remember the smell of the water, sour and salty, you know?"

"Sour?"

"Yeah. It's different," Jude trails off.

"Would you ever do it again?"

"Join the Navy? Hell no."

"I mean Italy. Would you ever visit again?"

"Oh. Yes. I'd like to see it again one day. Have you ever seen stars away from the city lights?"

"No."

Outside, the wind is pushing the swollen clouds, rattling my windows. Jude's voice is warm.

"It's beautiful. The night sky, and the stars. There are so many." Jude's voice dims. "I can still hear the waves pushing the anchor chains into the hull of our barge."

"It sounds calm."

"Not really, actually. When I think about it, the nights were stressful. I had to rig the slings into a big lift, and our lieutenant was always there, watching my every move. She gave me the creeps. Even the nights I wasn't on shift were a pain. God, the beds were awful. Imagine: thin mattresses stacked on these coffin racks with tattered curtains."

"The beds were awful," I repeat. "I like your story about the beach. Tell me about your time ashore."

"Okay"—Jude breathes out—"the street food is amazing. The paninis, filled with cheeses and fresh tomatoes. You've never had tomatoes this tasty."

"I can imagine," I lie.

"On my days off, I'd walk through the piazza. I'll never forget my first sip of espresso and tasting that moment of freedom—being away from home, being away from the barge. There was a one-room pub always full of men talking and drinking too much. That's where I usually ended up at the end of the day, when I had my free days, so by the time it was dark I'd be stumbling through the streets back to the barge. Happy to fall asleep."

"In your own bed?"

"Yes. My bed was fine when I was drunk or too tired to care and most of the time I was."

"Okay, now tell me about the beach."

"The hidden one?"

"Yes, I like that story."

"Okay, but then I need to get to bed. It's late."

And the wind howls in response.

"Every week we got one day off. This one day, I was wandering around and took a different route than usual. I came across the entrance to a small beach. It might have been privately owned. There was a couple lazing by the water and I spent hours with them, dipping in and out of the ocean, sipping their wine. Eventually, the man left and then the woman and I were all over one another."

I close my eyes, picture Jude kissing the sun-soaked woman. I can almost see it, almost feel it. The woman's legs wrapped around Jude and the sound of the sea. This picture, the one I imagine, is faded like one of Ghost's old photographs. I have seen the ocean but never yet tasted it or felt the salt water on my body.

"I like this part of the story," I whisper into the receiver.

"Which part?" I can hear Jude's smile.

One day, after I was diagnosed, before I understood what was happening, the world began to fade. It pulsed in and out. It wavered. And by the time I was aware and present again, everything had disappeared. Now, I have only Ghost's postcards. Small threads of information that are barely accessible. I understand that the beach has sun and sand and water. I know that this body enjoys sand and salty air. But the specific details, the important parts—those are missing.

"I want to go to the beach."

"Summer is close."

Jude yawns. "This other day I wandered into the empty piazza during *riposo*. It was my first time, and the streets were bare. I was so confused."

"But I want to hear more about the beach. What happened with the woman? Did you ever see her again?"

"No, it was brief," Jude says quickly, hoping to change topics.

☙

My first date with Jude is planned for mid-April. They've invited me to visit Seattle where, they say, we will sit across from the Great Wheel and sip small coffees. I cannot remember the Great Wheel. I know that I have visited once before. Years before my diagnosis, when the world was still vivid and clear.

Saturday afternoon, I catch the large boat from Victoria's Inner Harbour to Pier 69 in Seattle. The day is unusually warm for April. Everyone is discussing how fresh and humid the weather feels this early in the year. There is a man in a white button-up shirt and trousers pacing back and forth, stretching his legs in the aisle, loudly discussing business deals with a partner or friend into his cellphone. He is loud. There are families travelling on vacation, eating snacks, laughing, excitedly chirping to one another. Ghost is miserable. She misses the night ferries to Seattle when the only travellers were sleepy and quiet.

When I arrive, Jude is already on the platform, dressed in a crisp blue shirt and grey slacks. Their forehead glistens beneath their newsboy cap, but it is their eyes that I notice best. Like smooth silver stones with threads of colour—not quite blue or green. Still and calm.

As we walk I take in the big city. We are surrounded by buildings that swing upward, seemingly to defy gravity. Some heritage buildings are stout and constructed from broken stone, adding flavour to the grey metropolis.

We find some concrete steps away from the tourist area but still lending us a view. We sit in the sun, sipping dark coffee and watching the Great Wheel turn, again and again.

My voice cuts the silence. "Tell me about San Francisco."

Jude smirks, and their smile rides up my thighs.

"You see this scar?" They point to a thick whitish line above their brow. "This is SF now."

"I thought San Francisco was where all the queers live. I thought it was safe."

Jude sighs and shakes their head.

"It used to be. Lots of fights now. The tech bros ruined our safe haven. When I first moved to the Bay, it was filled with artists and queers. Folks that used to be outsiders, on the outskirts of society. SF was safe for us back then."

"You've been in lots of fights?" My throat tightens with excitement or confusion.

"Not really. Just that one night." Jude laughs.

I wonder if they can see my insides. See my heart pushing against my breasts, spilling blood into my cheeks.

"I was celebrating my friend's birthday. She was also leaving the Bay. All of her friends, we pretty much filled the bar. We were dancing, having a good time, when suddenly my friend Syd ran in and said a queer boy was getting beat up by some guys."

"Oh no ..."

"So, Syd and I ran outside, and there he was, couldn't be older than twenty-two. It was hard to tell. His face was ... there were three bros."

"Three?"

"Yep. My pal and I stepped in, blocked the kid from getting hurt any more, took a few punches. I don't remember much, but I took one in the nose and one above the eye. We made sure the kid was okay."

"Poor thing."

My coffee is nearly finished, the brown paper cup stained with lipstick. I slip my hand into Jude's.

"Sorry, my hands are so dry," they say.

"I like your hands." The air is sweet; there is an ice cream shop nearby. "I love the smell of sugar." I watch Jude's eyes soften.

Smoky-eyed Jude in the candied breeze, surrounded by skyscrapers.

"I would like to visit San Francisco one day. I'm not afraid."

Jude smirks. "Well, if you ever find yourself in SF and I'm there, I'll take you for coffee at Philz. It'll be the best coffee you'll ever have. The shop in the Mission is the best."

"Oh yeah?"

"Have you tried one-cup coffee before?"

"As in Starbu—"

"No, no. Philz isn't corporate at all. The founder created the business while he was working another job. He's like a coffee scientist." Jude's lips curve into a half smile. "It all happened years ago in a small liquor store in SF, and it's all hearsay, so don't quote me."

"Cross my heart."

Across the water, the Ferris wheel spins, its tiny metal benches swinging back and forth.

"He spent hours every day tinkering with these single-cup brewing machines, brewing cup after cup of coffee. Each cup with slight variations of spices and syrups, until he'd designed a list of different brews with the perfect flavour."

Jude looks almost proud.

"One day, I'd like to visit the Mission with you and try Philz." I say it like a promise.

The bloated afternoon sun is sinking into the water now, tracing colours across the horizon.

"Are you hungry?" Jude asks, their eyes tracing my own, catching my glance.

"Yes."

"How about we go back to my place? I have salmon and vegetables. You like fish, right?"

I link arms with Jude, to avoid holding hands. Even though the air is much cooler now, my hands are damp.

"Yes, I like salmon."

I know this for certain. Salmon is on my food list. It was one of
the first foods I added. I keep lists for most things now. Groceries,
personality traits, foods I enjoy, smells I enjoy. I have already filled all
the pages of two notebooks, mostly with lists repeating the same items
over and over again. My memory still needs work.

My new list is in a brown faux-leather notebook whose cover is
etched with golden swirls. The book was once Ghost's journal, its pages
dampened by lust, her cursive a beautiful trail of her memories. Tales
of escape to the east coast, the musty basement of a tattoo artist, sleeping in the Appalachian Mountains. When I read Ghost's words, this
heart aches for life, but that was before. Now, there are lists. Jagged
words whose letters disregard the ruled lines. I am building a person.

In my food list, I have scrawled the word *salmon*. It sits below
smoked paprika and above *chocolate cake*. Below *chocolate cake* is the
word *green*, and below that is the letter *A*.

I have been told that list keeping is good practice for me. That it
exercises my brain and my memory, is useful for working on writing
and gaining dexterity.

So, I make lists. I document who I am. Who I want to be.

The doctors tell me that my recovery will take time. My body is
filled with her thoughts. Ghost's photographs are ingrained in each
one of its cells. When I write lists, they are meant only for myself. The
lists are building me. They are my roads. I am beginning to know
what foods I enjoy, what smells comfort me, and what I desire.

But deep down, my Ghost says, "Don't you dare forget me."

CHAPTER 5

Jude's House

JUDE LIVES IN A STUDIO APARTMENT at the edge of Capitol Hill, across the street from a methadone clinic. They tell me that sometimes, late at night, a lone man screams all of his grievances into the moonlight. Jude has never seen him but understands why he's upset. They understand that Seattle is no longer a home for everyone.

"What happened in SF is happening in Seattle too, in Capitol Hill especially. This used to be the place for people who don't fit in. Now, it's being sold to the tech bros."

"Would you ever live in San Francisco again?"

Jude's brow furrows.

"No."

"Why not?"

"For the same reasons I explained to you before."

"Oh. Yes. Because of the tech bros?"

"No. Well, partly. I left in 2010 after the market crash. I was laid off and lost my benefits."

"I forget sometimes."

"I don't mind."

Jude makes their way to the tiny studio kitchen, its yellowed countertops pulsating under strong fluorescent lights. "I was forced to leave after the big economic collapse," they repeat.

They are pulling red salmon, lush greens, and thin bottles of liquid from the fridge.

"I was able to tease out a few more years, but it was a struggle. I couldn't afford even the basic necessities."

They are massaging oils into the fish. Buttering its slender body.

"My apartment had rent control, but without steady work or any benefits, the market crash was a game changer. I sold my car and bought a bike, a really nice light one that I rode all over town. Not even a month later, someone stole it out of the garage!"

Jude is a whirlwind in the kitchen. Their body swings from one area to the next.

"I remember now," I lie.

Remember this. I must remember all of this. San Francisco is "SF"; there is the Bay and the Mission District. Jude lived in the Lower Haight. They left after the big economic collapse, and the tech bros are dangerous.

The wooden spoon in Jude's hand clips around a large white bowl.

Save this scent, save these sounds.

"Why don't you pick a record to listen to?" Jude's eyes crinkle as they rinse off the spoon.

Warm spices fill the room as I make my way to the pinewood crate that holds Jude's records. Even though the crate has been sanded, threads of wood still hang off the edges.

"Any record?"

"Your choice."

In the crate, the bright record sleeves shine. They each promise an adventure. Their colours are confusing. I grab one and walk back to the kitchenette. Jude has finished prepping dinner and is now wiping the counter.

"Tina Turner. The queen of rock. Great choice. Have you used a turntable before?"

I shake my head.

"I'll set it up. My player is delicate. I've almost damaged it a couple of times myself. I think the needle is off centre."

I take a seat on the plush green sofa as a rich voice aches over the space.

"Have you heard this one before?"

I shake my head from side to side.

"This is one of my favourite albums," Jude says with a nod, handing me the album cover to look at.

By the time Jude and I sit down for dinner it is night. There is a slight draft from the windows, and the two small candles on the sill flicker.

Somewhere deep down, somewhere below my breastbone, I can feel Ghost getting restless. She doesn't appreciate how smoothly today went. She doesn't approve of people who are grounded because she thinks they are dull. She tells me it's the wild and passionate people who are experiencing life. Ghost is in love with someone else, so Jude will not do.

I take a bite of salmon, hope the fragrant spices will drown her frustrations.

"Would you like a sip?" Jude passes me their glass of whiskey.

"No thanks. I don't really drink much anymore."

Ghost doesn't like this either; she wants the glass, she wants the whole bottle.

"You don't mind if I do?"

"Not at all, please!"

Ghost isn't pleased.

I smile, take another bite of fish. "This is delicious, Jude, thank you."

&

After dinner, I hear the man who calls out his anguish to the stars. Jude and I are hidden beneath the sheets, snuggled into the deep, dark caves of one another.

"This is our first time, so let's take it slow," Jude whispers, their hand gently slipping between my thighs. I close my eyes.

I know that Ghost is enjoying Jude because my chest is no longer clenched, meaning her anger has faded. As Jude's lips trace the outline of my body, my breath catches. Ghost drums my heart until the room spins and I close my eyes.

"Are you all right?" Jude pulls back, their eyes muddled with concern.

"Yes," I assure them. "I think I'm just tired from the travel." I slip my hands up the sleeves of their T-shirt.

Jude's lips press against mine as Ghost's fingers reach down, down, down.

CHAPTER 6

Ghost and the Boy

ONCE UPON A TIME, Ghost was in love with a boy. They lived together on an island that floated at the edge of the sea. Their home was thin and flat, with floors made from wood that came from somewhere far away, deep within the forest.

The boy says that their building was old and funded by a non-profit agency for families just like theirs, and Ghost agrees. I know that the building was old because I stayed there for a short while. It was pieced together with bricks that each carried their own memories, and it had a long staircase with a floral-print carpet that reached all the way up to the boy's home.

Ghost and the boy each had their own bedrooms. While his was the colour of the sea, hers was the colour of eggs. She had four long windows that stretched up, up, up, almost to the ceiling. Across the street there was a brick church with a stained-glass window that shone brighter than any moon. In the evenings, as the sun dipped, I would stand in front of these windows and look at the short-stemmed trees with their spring leaves and the stained-glass window's pieces of coloured glass that shimmered in the fading light.

This church, on Gladstone Street, was used as a playhouse and so, on certain nights, people congregated outside of the entrance, beneath the stained-glass window. Ghost agrees that this is true. She has her own photographs of the playhouse. These were rich people, holding hands and filling the neighbourhood with excited chatter that danced up the side of the building and through the tall windows into Ghost's bedroom, in the house that she lived in with the boy she loved.

Ghost has memories of the boy that she has bundled with fat and crammed into my lymph nodes. Sometimes these memories prevent air from flowing freely into my lungs. The doctors call this anxiety, but they do not understand that the stress does not belong to me.

When Ghost remembers the boy, her fingers tap against my neck, and an old pain wraps its arms around my chest.

Ghost tells me that on the morning when she first met the boy, it was cold and festive. She stood on the ferry dock, which was golden beneath the winter sun, and the boy was waiting for her, as if they'd known each other for years. When Ghost drags me into her memory, the world drifts away until even the air disappears. Everything is frozen except for her and the boy.

That morning was gripped in time: the boy's hands folded over the steering wheel, his thin black tie illuminated by the street lamps. Ghost promises that when she first laid eyes on him, her heart screamed three octaves higher. She says that they professed their love under his creamy blond sheets, cheek to cheek, and that this thread between them held fast until her last day on earth.

But Ghost is wrong, again.

The boy listens as I flip through each photograph. He clicks his tongue and adjusts each frame until the story is honest. The boy is truth, because his memory is pristine, his mind is still his own.

"When I first saw your picture, I thought you looked fun. Happy."

"My picture online?"

"Yeah."

"And I came to visit you?"

"It was right after New Year's and bloody cold. Streets were icy. And yeah, you were just like I thought you would be."

"It was cold that day. Yes, I remember."

The boy and Ghost met in the middle of winter, when the streets were slippery with frost.

"You drove me through downtown, right?" My ears are piqued as I balance the phone on my shoulder.

"Yeah. You know, when I first met you, I actually thought you talked too much. I was worried it would annoy me!" He laughs.

"What did I talk about?"

"Just ... everything. Like I said, you talked tons."

"And after a while it didn't bother you?"

"Well, it did sometimes, but just 'cause I'm an introvert. It wasn't all bad. You were happy with me back then, so I didn't mind."

"So, it was cold?"

Ghost is right about this part. Her breath steams as the ferry docks.

"Yeah, and bloody late. You and your friend caught the last ferry."

And then Ghost sighs and begins repainting her tale of that night while she listens to the boy. The ferry is docking. The dark streets shimmer with frost beneath the street lamps.

"I was wearing a long jacket that night."

"Yeah, I think so."

And Ghost begins digging, her thin fingers poking my lymph nodes, until each memory surfaces.

"I was with Bobbi."

"That's right."

"My jacket was black with large buttons. And Bobbi's hair was bubble-gum pink. I met you outside. It was cold."

"We met in the parking lot. I was still driving my beater, and Jesse was still crashing on my sofa."

"I remember now."

Ghost in her long jacket and the boy's eyes on the ferry dock. And then Ghost sings; her high-pitched squeal dislodges another part of the story. Ghost and the boy are facing one another, breath visible. It is night. The boy told Ghost this part of the story once before, a long time ago. He said that when he and Ghost first hugged, he knew that this was forever.

Still, Ghost has a different picture. It's as if she captured her favourite season and dressed each memory in a golden warmth, laced all the different periods into one long season. I suppose the night is dark enough for her. She hides these postcards in muscles and tendons. She has buried herself in many of these cells. But, like I said, these are lies. Ghost promises that this boy held her heart. She has buried memories of him somewhere deep, somewhere safe. I can feel them somewhere below my tongue. In her favourite picture, the boy is wearing a sleeveless black shirt with something scrawled across the chest. The air is quiet. Everything is frozen. The wind does not breathe here. Ghost is half-naked, her body wrapped in a blue quilt, fingers curved around a dark porcelain mug of sweetened coffee. Her other hand balances a cigarette. Next to her on the brown sofa sits the boy. His shoulders are straight, held back proudly, and he is smiling. The sun has kissed everything.

This was before he transitioned and before you were diagnosed. Before I was diagnosed. This is while you still were lost in the poetry of young love.

Yes, Ghost tells me, she has been in love only once.

She tells me that when she first laid eyes on the boy, the world drifted away. Her eyes and her red lips. The boy's hands gripping the steering wheel. His thin black tie. The warmth of the afternoon as his car rumbled down the street. The trees calling at the sky.

This is before the first snowfall of the season, sometime in the early afternoon, during a bout of wet freshness that was typical of that time of year. Already, the trees were heavy with dew, and a warm haze hung over the road. His truck pushes onward, as a static beat from the car radio cuts through the scene. This is before the hospital. Before that day in November.

"Forget me not," Ghost's tune plays over the radio, as the boy's car rumbles on into the afternoon sun.

CHAPTER 7

San Francisco

THE SUN BURNS BRIGHT as Jude and I catch an airplane to the Bay. Airplanes frighten me. It is difficult to believe in the safety of such a heavy object carrying me over the clouds, but Jude promises me that we will not be a statistic.

"It's actually really rare for planes to crash. It's a one in six million chance. You have a higher chance of being struck by lightning."

"What are the chances of being struck by lightning?" I ask, my hands clasping the plastic handle on my suitcase.

"Slim." Jude is studying their boarding pass. "Gate c-22, and we're at A-10 ..."

The airport is filled with people, their voices ringing in brightly lit stores and stands selling chocolates, perfume, hats, and T-shirts. Products that act as time capsules for people to capture their journey, to take it home.

"Do you have my boarding pass?"

"I have your boarding pass and your headphones. I think c-22 is this way." Jude begins walking slowly.

"Jude? If our plane crashes and we die, it'll be quick, right?"

"Yes, but there's only a slim chance. Okay, the numbers are going backward, so this is the right way. Wait, no, this is D—I think we have to turn around."

"Quick, as in no suffering. I don't want to feel my body on fire or choke to death on smoke."

Jude turns to face me, their eyes just grey today. Sweet, sugary grey.

"Listen, the chances of a plane accident are less than getting struck by lightning or hit by a car walking down the street. If the plane does crash, it's safest to be seated at the rear of the plane."

"And that's where we are?"

"Yep. That's why I always choose the back of the plane. Okay, this is definitely the wrong way. We have to hurry now."

"I wish we could have driven."

"I do usually drive to the Bay. The coast is beautiful. I wish we had the time, but I only have four vacation days left."

⚘

The seats on the plane are a dusty blue with a pattern of curvy maroon shapes. Bruised moons. Jude booked us in this rear section of the plane because it's considered the safest.

Even so, my stomach is in knots.

As the massive engines growl to life, my chest aches, and my fingers wrap around Jude's wrist.

"The takeoff always scares me too." Jude pulls my hand into their large one, holding it like a rare bird. "Close your eyes. Deep breaths."

As the plane starts to move, my heart skips into my throat.

"Close your eyes. Deep breaths," Jude repeats.

I think of the purple moon, the faded blue seat. I breathe. If I am going to die now, let it be quick. No pain.

Somewhere below my ribcage, Ghost is wailing, her sharp teeth digging into my shoulders, forcing me to hunch forward until my neck disappears, until my chin meets my chest. My fingers grip the plastic arms of the seat.

"It's all right," I hear Jude say. "Just close your eyes. This is a short flight."

Their words pull me close and relax me a little as the plane lifts off the ground. A shooting star taking off into the clouds, so high that everything down below seems non-existent. Meanwhile, Ghost continues to drag her jagged teeth along the bones of my shoulder, until a slow burning erupts there.

I breathe into my chest, let Jude's warmth blanket me and suffocate Ghost.

"There's a café two blocks from my old place in the Lower Haight," Jude says. "And I know the owner, Ginger. It's laid back with comfy old sofas and all these colourful tapestries on the walls."

"I like the sound of that." I nuzzle in deeper.

"And she remembers everyone's name. She'd always ask how I was doing when I came in. She really cared about people."

"I hope I get to meet her."

"If her place is still running, we'll go there and I'll introduce you, okay?"

Jude's breath is slow and even; their chest rises and falls gently.

"I'd like that," I say, squeezing their hand.

❧

Jude has arranged for us to stay in their old apartment in the Lower Haight. The street swells with life. Fast cars and graffiti, sun-drenched people, restaurants boasting rich smells that tickle your throat. In the early morning, Jude says, the scent of fresh bread from the bakery across the street whispers through the windows, under the door cracks. The buildings in San Francisco remind me of cake, their bodies decorated with ornate architecture and slathered in frosted colours—raspberry, marigold, buttercup. If San Francisco were a bird, it would be a macaw.

"My old apartment is on the third floor," Jude says, pointing up at a yellow building with peeling paint.

"It's kind of your friend to let us stay," I say as we make our way up the concrete stairs.

"Mia doesn't mind. She's staying with her girlfriend while we visit."

Jude gave Mia the apartment after they lost their job and decided to leave San Francisco, under the condition that Mia would give it back to Jude if they ever returned to SF.

The one-bedroom apartment is small, with high ceilings and a gas heater below the bay windows. There are several prints of different Frida Kahlo self-portraits, including one with parrots.

After Jude finishes unpacking, they take my hand and lead me to the back of the apartment. "I want to show you the backyard. It's really special."

Behind the building is a small patch of grass with dozens of plants. Thick plants with leaves like tongues, painted with dew. Plants with fanned leaves like a peacock's tail.

A car horn sounds. I enjoy the noise of a city. The constant movement and celebration. The colours, the greenery. In the city, Ghost's wails are accompanied by life. In the city, she is never alone. My nose tingles with the scent of baked bread and spice.

My eyes are saucers. I can feel my pupils dilating with serotonin. "I want to live here with you one day," I tell Jude.

Jude's palm curves over the small of my back.

"Remember, love, the city has changed. It'll always be nice to visit, but I can't live here again. We'll find another city."

The plants listen, their bodies bending under the weighted air as the fog rolls in.

Ghost doesn't notice the beauty of SF. She is still wailing, lost in her own memories of cities played out in bent keys, a broken flute, a shrieking chorus. To her, SF is paved with fun, and I am stiff. She grabs my ear and whispers of her time in someone else's truck, winding down the road in West Virginia, the sun beating across the dash. And then, in the same truck, rumbling through a waterlogged street beneath a storm, flashes of lightning and the deep rumble of thunder overhead. Her first taste of sweet tea and how it coated her lips. The person driving the truck was breathless over the loss of someone important. Ghost, much like that lost person, would be leaving soon herself.

Jude's arm drapes over my shoulders, smothering Ghost's tales. "How about I introduce you to Philz now?"

"The best coffee I'll ever have?"

"You can tell me what you think." They smile.

After the sun collapses, when darkness softens the room, conversations from passersby slip up the side of the building, fill the room, and remind us that we are not alone.

"When I lived here, I could always hear couples arguing on their way home from the bar. Every weekend I'd overhear at least one breakup. So many nights at three a.m., couples would be fighting and crying directly outside, hashing out their entire relationship on my front stoop."

"It is a good stoop."

"So, lots of times, especially on the weekend, I'd pop my head out the window and tell people to hash out their mess somewhere else."

I can picture one of the couples now. Her hair scented with another's lust. I can imagine it because maybe I have seen this before myself.

"I used to live across the street from a bar," I tell Jude.

"So, you understand the late-night frustration," Jude says, eyes gleaming.

"During my last summer in the house, there was a new owner, or maybe he just worked there. After the pub was closed, he'd stand right under my bedroom window to show off his motorcycle."

"Every night?"

"Every weekend after midnight. It was the same routine every time. The street would be quiet and still for a while, but as soon as I closed my eyes to sleep, the drunken hoots started. His voice was always the loudest. He and his friends always sang the same Journey song."

"Journey is exhausting."

"Then, after they repeated the chorus a million times, he'd start revving the engine and they'd just holler. This would go on for about an hour ... every weekend."

"I'm glad you don't sing Journey."

I nod. Wrap my arms around Jude's neck and kiss their cheek.

"Or hoot and holler."

"I'm glad you don't have a loud motorbike."

"You're a quiet bird." Jude smiles.

"I like the quiet now. I like the calm. Maybe I'm old."

My chest tightens, and I can feel Ghost stirring against my ribcage. She is awake now. Her fingers are tapping against my sternum. She must be looking for memories.

"We all change every few years, right?" Jude says with a laugh.

"Right."

Ghost wails. Her cries are clogging my ears. When this happens, I stretch my mouth into an *O* shape and force a yawn. It sometimes helps. Other times, I plug my nose and blow to make a small popping sound. The doctors recommend these and other manoeuvres to help my ears. They say that the loud cries are tinnitus, which can be brought on by neurological changes. Brain trauma.

⁂

The following afternoon, Jude and I drive our rental car to a secret beach north of the Mission District. The white sand beach is a secret because only people staying at the hotel adjacent to it have access. All along the rocky seawall is a chicken-wire fence with wooden signs that read Private. Jude helps me over the wire fence, holding first my coffee, then my hand. My feet slip on the fence, barely gripping the metal, which shakes beneath my weight.

North of the Mission, the wind is cooler. It ripples up my shirt sleeves, kissing my biceps until my arms are covered in scaly goosebumps.

I grasp Jude's shoulder and press my body into theirs, desperate to capture some heat.

"It's freezing!" I say with a laugh.

The wind, in response, pushes our bodies closer.

"You are a tiny bee and I am a tank," Jude says as my hair tangles around both our necks. The sky is an unmarked stale blue.

Jude is right: they are a tank. Their frame is sturdy. They are armoured, immovable, even in the heaviest of storms.

⁂

After the beach, we drive the rental Kia along the shoreline to Jude's favourite seaside diner. It's a tiny building painted cream and blue. Dried starfish decorate the door, their desiccated bodies stuck to the door frame. Some are missing legs or arms, skeletal reminders of the mortality we all face.

Inside the diner, the old wooden chairs groan as Jude and I sit down.

A lady saunters up to the table, her cheeks radiant even under the yellow lights.

"We're here for the crab legs—a big basket. And water." Jude grins at her.

"Big basket coming up! You hear that, Gale?" she calls to the kitchen. "I'll be back with your waters."

She swivels to the kitchen, her ponytail swinging slightly as she shifts her weight.

"I haven't done this in a while. I used to eat here every summer after the beach. Everything's still the same." Jude's eyes shimmer with creases of hazel as they settle back into their chair.

"Did you come here by yourself?"

"Yes, it was a private adventure. I think personal trips are important, don't you?"

"I think so, yes."

Before long, the lady brings us a basket of fresh crab's legs. My stomach is grumbling as I reach into the basket.

"Careful," Jude warns. "They're hot."

I lean back against my groaning wooden chair and let Jude fill my plate with crab legs. I watch them crack and peel back the shells with ease.

It is still light out, though the temperature is beginning to drop, which means that the fog will come soon.

"Take a bite!" Jude says, watching me with excitement.

I reach for a small fork and jab it into the crab flesh.

"Don't forget to butter it."

I dip the piece of white flesh into a metal ramekin full of butter. The meat falls off my fork and sinks to the bottom. I fish the crabmeat out with my fork and pop it into my mouth.

"There are some things I miss about living here." Jude's voice sounds distant.

"I miss lots of things too," I agree.

"Things from ...?"

"From before."

Jude looks at me, their eyes wide. "Do you think you've changed a lot since your surgery?" Their voice is soft.

"I don't know." My lips are oily. I can taste salt and the sea. "It's like a hazy dream. I still need to find out what happened back then."

"Your mom knows, right? Your friends?"

"She was away for most of it. It all happened on the Island. It seems like such a long time ago."

"Have you spoken to your doctor?"

"About my memory? No. I do have one person ... He remembers."

Jude looks toward the window. "Fog's coming in."

I pull on my cardigan to cover the fresh goosebumps.

&

It is dusk by the time Jude and I arrive back at the yellow building. In the backyard, we rest our swollen bellies against the grass.

"I want to go to Portugal with you and swim in the Mediterranean," Jude says.

I'm mesmerized by Jude's knowledge of the world.

"Me too. I want to do those things."

"And we'll eat fresh cheese on the beach."

"And olives. The big ones."

"I want to relax with you. Just me and you."

"Just me and you," I sing, as Ghost begins to stir.

CHAPTER 8

Dreams

IT IS ALREADY OUR LAST NIGHT in San Francisco, and Jude and I are lying next to one another on Mia's bed, skin to skin. The sun has already collapsed into the ocean, and the scent of salty dampness creeps through the crack under the door.

"Are you asleep?" Jude whispers, just as I'm slipping into the dark.

"Almost," I mumble into their chest, breathing in their musky cologne. Outside of this room, cars zoom by. The deep stereo bass they're playing collides with Ghost's faint wails, until the sound is a reminder of something I can't quite grasp, a distant taste of something I once tried, a very long time ago.

"I'm not used to all of this traffic anymore," Jude says.

Their body is warm and comforting. I think of the bright stuccoed buildings, the bustling streets.

"Earplugs?"

"Didn't bring them, remember?"

The ambience of cars zooming past settles peacefully into all the darkened areas of the bedroom.

Jude sighs.

Ghost stirs.

Whenever Ghost listens to music, she sings along. Her songs find a home in all the distant parts of me, the parts that only she can see. I feel her digging through my body, attempting to unearth the memories she has buried. Tiny Ghost, clad in soil, searching, searching for proof that she is still alive. She uncovers memories beneath my tongue, wrapped in veins and vessels, and when I am tired, while I'm asleep, she reminds me.

"I want to marry you someday," Jude whispers and kisses my cheek. And I curl in deeper. "But not in a church. I want it to be in the forest, surrounded by trees."

I picture the trees with red and yellow leaves and dark soil that smells of cedar.

"Yes, with tiny lights like fireflies." My voice is distant as the dark opens its own mouth and invites me in.

"Churches aren't romantic," Jude continues. I listen to their chest filling with air, rising, then slowly deflating. "My mom used to force me to go to Sunday school at the priest's house. It was a small house surrounded by a cornfield."

"The priest was a corn farmer?"

"No, He just lived there. I don't know why. My mom would drive me there on Sundays after church. I'd always dash out of her car and hide in the cornstalks, and my mom would get so angry and say I was being difficult. Everyone else loved the priest, but I didn't trust him. I knew there was something wrong with him."

Jude's breathing is deep and relaxed.

"And?"

"We found out some things later and he left the Church."

"Where is he now?"

"I don't know. I was right, though. I knew that he was dangerous."

Jude's stomach rises and falls. Rises and falls. Their breath is the wind from earlier, their arms wrapped around me, holding my frame, creating warmth, guiding me into the dark where Ghost lives. Somewhere deep and far beyond. Somewhere hidden. When I sleep, Ghost's memories blossom like hungry flowers. She has buried her own tale about a church deep within my bone marrow. A dried memory, not quite forgotten. It lives in the dark with Ghost in the place of Almost. While I am asleep, Ghost and I visit. She takes my hand and whispers stories. She shows me photographs and films. I wander from place to place with her, take note of who she was. Record the tales she tells me through each one of her buried pieces.

CHAPTER 9

The Church

TONIGHT, GHOST IS DESPERATE. Her fingernails, sharpened like campfire sticks, puncture my palm as she pulls me deeper into the darkness. Because the avenues here are unmarked, I grip her hand, allowing her fingernails to slice me. Allowing her to weave me through the paths.

Tonight, she has no photographs. It is completely dark. Until she finds the right place, and we wait. We wait until small bits of light form. We wait until her memory is crisp. We sit along a tree branch, watching the empty landscape, as Ghost calmly swings her legs back and forth, humming a tune unknown to me. As the night begins to clear, the sky burns gold. Roadways below are stamped across the horizon.

On a concrete hill, there is a church bearing a lonely cross on its slanted roof. From our spot in the tree at the bottom of the hill, we watch. Nearby is a narrow townhome with a cream-coloured door, a bronze door handle, and perfectly manicured bushes and freshly mown grass out front.

Ghost slithers down the tree. The wind is calm and silent. I don't feel like moving. My body is exhausted. So, I sleep. I rest my head against the tree trunk and close my eyes. I hear the soft flapping of cards in bike wheel spokes and the crunch of gravel.

Ghost rides her canary-yellow bicycle past the church at the top of the hill. I am on the back of the bicycle, my arms wrapped around her bony chest. We bike up the hill, Ghost's legs wobbling. The tires are low on air, the rubber handlebars are well loved. I can tell it is Sunday because people in suits and dresses are standing in front of the church. They are clean, translucent. They glow. The women wear pearl necklaces and long pencil skirts. Their children speak softly.

To the right, near the entrance of the church, there is a woman who seems familiar. She catches Ghost's eye too. The woman wears a sea-green skirt and matching jacket. She reminds me of movie star.

Ghost rides her bike up and down the laneway, staring at the churchgoers with curiosity. They stare back at us. On the horizon, the sun gradually dips back into the earth. Fluorescent street lamps switch on and buzz like June bugs. Soon, the church parking lot is empty, except for one car hidden in the back corner.

Ghost and I ride over to the car, and she grabs my wrist and smiles because this is her story about a church.

Smoke gasps out of the car's tailpipe, curling up toward the stars, as Ghost climbs off her bicycle and saunters up to the car. The night wraps around me, pushes me forward, until Ghost and I are pressed right up against one another, my stomach pushing against the bones in her spine. There is a guy with a blue faded hat and bleached blond hair sitting in the car. A smooth tune rides through the open window.

Now Ghost is holding my hand and holding his shoulder.

"Hey Druid," she says with a smile as she reaches into her purse and pulls out a pack of cigarettes.

He smirks. "Shit. guess what I found out? My family has a castle in Scotland. You and I could go there one day, yeah?"

"Maybe." Ghost smiles, slips her fingers under the door handle, and pulls.

"My mom and dad are there right now. I'm gonna go once I'm all finished with my research." Druid tilts his seat back and leans his body forward. His car is musty, with seats that cough up small particles of dust.

"Oh yeah?" Ghost climbs in and sits down.

Druid's face is solemn, his pudgy cheeks growing pinker as all words tumble from his mouth.

"Yeah. Things are getting pretty busy at the lab."

Ghost rolls her window down and lights up her smoke without speaking, turns her head away from Druid.

"I don't mind if you smoke. I could help you quit, if you want. I once wrote a self-help guide on bad habits."

Ghost smirks and shrugs her shoulders.

The church parking lot is dark, except for a thin patch of ground illuminated by the yellow glare of the street lamps. They talk some more. His name isn't Druid. It's Dustin or Denver. He listens to pop-punk. Ghost knows that he is strange, that he lies.

"You're so different," he says with a smile. "Do you want to go out again sometime? A date? Maybe next weekend? Maybe tonight? Do you know any bars around here?"

Ghost is bored. His stories are dull.

"I don't have ID," she says.

"I know a guy who does the best IDs."

"Maybe. I'm going home now." Ghost leans over and kisses him. Stains his lips with hers. Steals the taste of gin from his mouth.

He gently places his hand on her shoulder.

"Look," he whispers, glancing down.

He has unzipped his fly and exposed himself.

Ghost shoves his shoulder, turns her body, and kicks the door open.

Her sneakers pound the cement of the parking lot. She screams in laughter as his car squeals out of the lot. As it rumbles down the laneway. Far away from her.

Near the entrance of the church, where the movie star woman had been standing, Ghost pauses for a moment. Then runs back to her bike, jumps on, pedals furiously into the dark. I imagine myself in the Hollywood woman's silk blouse and pencil skirt. She is probably asleep right now, as it's well past midnight. She would never spend her evenings smoking with random men or kissing people as a friendly goodbye, and she would probably avoid Ghost.

Ghost passes the church and follows the wide road to her own street.

✿

I can still taste Druid's lips as my body begins to stir from sleep. I can still taste the memory of gin as I press against Jude's chest. Their body is hot and close. It is still early, and the sky is barely lit. Outside, a dog barks, someone laughs, a car drives by, and then another one, and then another. Jude has booked our flight home for later this afternoon, so there is time. Time to walk the streets of the Haight and to visit Chinatown.

Jude is still asleep, their body calm, uninhabited.

"Jude?" I whisper.

They shift, roll toward me, and pull me closer.

"Last night I dreamt about this church by my old house." I mumble into their chest, letting their scent speak of home.

"Mm-hmm."

"And this lady who looked like a movie star and a boy who pulled down his pants. I kissed him goodbye and ran away. I can still taste his lips."

Jude's eyes are open now, ashy warm with bits of light.

"I think this happened when I was younger."

In the street below, a car squeals and honks aggressively.

"I asked you not to share sex dreams with me, remember?"

"I wasn't attracted to the boy in my dream ..."

"I'm not comfortable with hearing about your sex dreams. It's not what I want to wake up to on our first vacation together, can you understand that?" Jude replies.

Jude is right. I think they have mentioned this before, after I shared another dream from Ghost. Her dreams, her memories, make Jude uncomfortable. They make me uncomfortable. Jude has asked me this more than once. I must remember. Who would enjoy having to repeat themselves about something like this? I must remember.

Jude gets up from the bed.

"I'm sorry," I call over as they exit the room.

Ghost folds her bony hands over my shoulder blades and begins to wail. I know that she is pleased with Jude's reaction. She doesn't wish for anyone else to be a part of our world.

I, on the other hand, am lonely.

CHAPTER 10

Ghost's Island

 WHEN GHOST SINGS OF HER HOME, stories of the Island blossom. A small and hidden dream, tucked away in the middle of the sea. Her chords screech across the landscape, telling me of home and the boy. She builds a timeline, unearthing herself, explaining that the ripples of pain in my lower back are from months of sleeping on wiry sofas.

Her journal entries paint pictures of the night she watched rain clouds from a concrete rooftop somewhere on the east coast, or when she stained her palms with the red sands of Arizona desert, or lay beneath a lemon tree in the backyard of some beautiful actor's home in California. That was years ago, though, when Ghost was still young, still trying to find her home.

On the day I decide to leave her island, the clouds hang heavy over the road, threatening to burst as I dial Mama's number. Ghost holds her breath and listens to me talking to her mama, hears me say that I belong on the mainland, that really, the city ashore is my home.

"Yes, yes. And your doctors are closer, just in case," her mama agrees.

Jude appreciates my decision as well. "Good news. I'll help you pack, birdie."

And, in response, Ghost shrieks and rails her bony fists against my chest until my lungs rattle, because none of this was her decision.

It is nearing the end of the month when Jude catches a ferry to the Island. They kiss my cheek, roll up their sleeves, and begin care-fully wrapping plates in newspaper pages, tying elastic bands around silverware, and tossing mousetraps in the back-alley Dumpster. I pack boxes with pans and the paper-wrapped plates. I fold towels, edge to edge, and place them in another box with the glasses, because Jude says towels are free padding. They know this because, like Ghost, they have lived in a number of places and moved many times.

When the box is full, I tape it closed, marking it with a *K* for kitchen. Most of the other boxes are marked with an *M* for miscellaneous, because there aren't many boxes, and after Kitchen, the items don't have a particular place—except for the ones in Ghost's box, which I've secretly filled with her old journals, photographs, and a few T-shirts. She is still crying as I tape it closed and place it, unmarked, beneath my other household boxes.

"Almost done," I tell Jude, and they kiss me, because we both hope that being almost done means the past is finished, and the rest of my story will place in the present moment. Their palm rubs my belly, face entangled in my wild mane, and we listen to the evening chorus of busy mice, who soon pause their work because they are curious about the different sounds around my home.

The night before I leave for the mainland, I say goodbye to the Island. Ghost and I walk past a sweet-smelling garden and a quiet school field. We walk up the block, past the grocery store, past the bar filled with weeknight patrons, to the boy's home, where Ghost once lived. Upstairs, the lights are still on: the boy is awake.

Ghost pulls at my lips and crams her foot up my neck, filling my throat, stealing my air.

"I'm sorry," I whisper, and continue walking down the sidewalk. The sidewalk that Ghost stumbled over that morning, when the clouds were a rosy pink. We pass a schoolyard and a bus stop. As always, the streets here are quiet as the sky melts behind the shadowed homes.

These days, I live in the city on the mainland, in a small apartment on a tree-lined street close to the hospital. My balcony welcomes brown-breasted birds instead of seagulls and busy mice. Each street bustles with busy people going about their days. Ghost misses her island. She paints memories of the Island and the boy and their home across my bones. I know that the mainland is better for me. It is filled with my own desires, not Ghost's.

Jude brings me a housewarming gift of plants. We spend most of the weekend scrubbing the grey concrete balcony and tossing out a cracked, dusty chandelier that is beyond hope. We lay out faux-wood tiles and seafoam-blue plant pots etched with thick lines. Bright-green leaves spill over the ledge. Spaced between each pot are thick, gnarled branches from a hike Jude took along the beach near the Bay, months before we met. On the old metal railing, we twine small globe lights, and above it, we place a small hanging bird bath. Now, throughout the year, sweet, tiny birds visit my home, splashing in the shallow metal dish, then digging their strong beaks into the soil and unearthing seeds and roots for their homes.

The city on the mainland is constructed of rows of concrete: tall buildings and tiny trees, some with gentle lights that look like June bugs. Here, thousands of people live, all in a rush. Ghost dislikes this. The constant noise makes her agitated. She tosses and turns until my heart feels dislodged and my eyes are swimming in confusion. She sings about salty waves and gentle streets.

I call the boy from my home on the mainland, and while I watch the brown-breasted birds hop across my balcony garden, I ask him to tell me about Ghost, to remind me of that day in November.

He is smoking. I can hear him inhale, then exhale. He is nervous. His voice is quiet.

"Afterward, you were angry a lot. Mainly at me."

Ghost shakes her head. "I love him!" she shrieks.

"It was the pills, I think," I say.

"I don't know. Even after the pills. Everything was different."

"Do you think I'm still different?"

"Wouldn't know," he mumbles. Inhale and exhale.

I want to tell him that he is a ghost now, but I don't know how to say it.

CHAPTER 11

The Rain

IN SEATTLE, WHERE JUDE LIVES, the winter wind curls its icy legs around the city and drowns the soft greenery in buckets of rain. On days like this, when the rain continues for hours, the streets fill with water, and a shallow moat forms around Jude's apartment building. Inside, we warm our toes with woollen socks. When it rains, Jude and I spend our weekends in their apartment, dreaming of the summer months, heating our lips with cups of sugared coffee and then with one another.

Jude's windowsills are decorated with small succulent plants and a few larger plants with long leaves that dance when the windows vibrate from the wind, when wild gusts sweep down the alley and over the roof of the methadone clinic to smash against the outer wall of Jude's cozy studio apartment.

"Seattle is miserable," Jude says, again and again, and most of the time I agree with them. Meanwhile, San Francisco is bright, sugary, lively.

"Do you miss San Francisco?"

"I don't really, like I told you. The Bay is different now—big companies, tech bros."

"Oh yes. It is pretty, though."

"Ever since Amazon moved in, Capitol Hill is the same as SF now. Cities in general are all being crushed by tech companies."

"Tell me about how San Francisco used to be."

Jude sighs. "It used to be for people like us—the artists, the queers, the ones who needed a place to call home."

"Are you all right?"

But Jude is in the kitchen now, mixing a drink, and their small cat is calling for food.

Rain keeps plummeting from the sky, creating a stream that flows from one end of the alley to the other. The wind begins calling. Small howls that are barely noticeable over Jude's blues record. We sit at the table. Jude pours themself a short glass of Scotch and adds three drops of bitters and two big cubes of ice.

"That looks good," I say, trying to mend whatever is broken, whatever is missing.

"Do you want a sip?"

"No. But I want to smell it."

Jude passes me their drink and I breathe it in, my nostrils collecting the intoxicating body of the brew.

"I added bitters to this one, can you tell the difference?"

"Yes, maybe."

"Scotch with bitters reminds me of this place in the Mission where my friends and I would go. We felt at home there before they shut it down. It was walking distance from my place at the time."

I picture the foggy streets of the Mission District and a tiny bar, half hidden by the fog, where Jude and their friends shared tales about love, political turmoil, and the classist suits of the world.

I know why Jude is sad these days. It's the rain. In San Francisco, the sky is clear until late afternoon, when the fog emerges. Rain is sadder. But Jude and I keep each other warm.

"Are you ready?" they ask.

"Yes."

I take a small sip of water, and then I do it again, not because I am thirsty but because it seems as though I should. Jude has set out a small plate of snacks for me. Strawberries with their stems removed, sliced in four pieces, and evenly spread over a paper towel to soak up the juice and ensure the pieces are easy to pick up. Sliced cheese in perfect rectangles with wheat crackers. These are gifts to let me know that they care, small love notes to assure me that I am no longer alone.

"You can go first." Jude places the dice in front of me.

When we play dice, we do not use a calculator. Jude says that this is good for our brains. They say that brain exercise ensures our minds stay healthy. Dice is a game that exercises our brains. It is good for arithmetic. We roll six dice. Watch them land. There are specific combinations that earn you points. The game is based on luck. Jude is able to add the numbers quickly; they do so in a matter of seconds. They look at the dice and have an answer. I need more time. I realize that my difficulty with addition is not due to lack of practice. I want to tell Jude that my brain has different issues, that I have been haunted since that day in November. That my body is a vessel shared by me and Ghost, and I am the uninvited guest. If my brain was once able to complete mathematical equations in a matter of seconds, it no longer can. Instead, the neural pathways are filled with Ghost's conflicting stories, her tiny wails and pulsating colours.

But instead, I nod.

"Mommy needs a new pair of slippers!" Jude laughs as I roll the smooth plastic dice and watch all of them bounce off the wooden table with a snap. Too many dice. Their bodies gleam in the light of the table lamp.

"I want my calculator."

"Try without first." Jude's eyes are on the dice, their pencil hovering over the sheet of paper.

I watch the dice and wait. Wait for something to click.

"Let's do this in sections," Jude offers, pushing three dice toward me.

"Two and two and two is six," I count aloud.

"Yep."

Jude pushes the remaining three dice forward.

"Three and one and one is five."

"Mm-hm. Now add those together."

Jude's short glass catches the light.

Six plus five.

Five and five is ten, so six and five must be eleven.

"Eleven?"

"Yep, good job. You'll get better. We'll play dice a lot." Jude smiles and takes another sip from their glass.

"I want to use the calculator."

"It just takes practice. Your brain needs the practice."

And they are right, my brain does need the practice, so I take another sip from my water glass and nod while Ghost pushes her weight onto my bladder and whines.

Sometimes when it rains, Jude and I drive up to the northern belt of Seattle proper. We whiz by huge pine trees and colonial homes with wide wooden steps and glossy windows.

Sometimes Jude will slow the car to a crawl alongside a home and point to a well-lit driveway and say, "We could afford one of these if we got a mortgage. I've reviewed most of the rates in Seattle, and there's better opportunity out here, farther north."

And I say, "These houses are beautiful."

"One day, babe. One day, we can live here."

Jude understands investments and saving pennies. Their sturdy green Ford is always polished and smells of paper. Clean and comforting. They say that their car may not be expensive like other people's, but it still takes us wherever we need to go. They say that people who spend more than they need to on a car have low self-esteem.

Tonight, the rain is pelting against the windows, and the wind is howling through the small cracks in the door frame. The brief moments of daylight offer a lazy orange glow. Because it is almost winter, the sun burns modestly, even when the wet cold is freezing my bones and nothing is dry enough to catch fire. Yes, even then, the quiet light flashes momentarily before it fades. I watch the last remaining strokes of orange and red.

CHAPTER 12

Ghost and the Rain

MAMA SAYS THAT WHEN GHOST WAS YOUNGER, algebra was her favourite subject because it read like an unspeakable language, but once learned, all questions could be answered. Every other evening after sunset, after John had left the house with his large canvas bag and taped hockey stick to meet the guys, Ghost and Mama would practice equations. These slippery memories are hidden beneath my right molar, close enough to the nerve endings for me to feel but distant enough for me to note that these stories are from long ago.

As Ghost walks me to the house, we clasp hands. Caught in the gasp of summer's breeze, we pass a large black dog tied to a laundry line who growls as we walk up Ghost's wide driveway. Wild blackberries creep over the fence surrounding the yard, their jagged leaves dressed in the dew.

And then Ghost leads me into her home. She shows me the table in the hallway where we are to take off our sneakers and tiptoe quietly over the brown rug, to the kitchen with its creamy curtains and softly painted roses on the walls.

The kitchen is quiet. In here, it is a warm, breathless day. All of her memories are frozen. The checkered countertops glow in the sunlight, and a warm halo rests above her head.

Tiny Ghost. She is young here; she shrinks and morphs until she is the size of my pinky finger.

We sit on the brown-leather banquette with the grainy tile underfoot and watch as Ghost's mama holds up flash cards with mathematical equations on them.

"Five plus six is?" Mama asks.

Without a beat, Ghost snaps her fingers and says with a giggle, "Eleven."

"Such a smart little thing," I whisper, and Mama agrees, because she nods her head with pride and her honeyed eyes gleam. The whole kitchen seems to glow as well.

Ghost's story is thin and therefore it does not, cannot take up much room. The vision doesn't play out for very long. The colours fade out. The kitchen cabinets, the table, the leather banquette, all collapse into nothingness. Outside, the sun dims until there is just a warm dark space where it was.

"Such a smart little thing," I whisper. The darkness breathes me in and spits me out on the damp concrete of a city sidewalk beside an older Ghost with hot-pink hair and a nose ring. We sit on the curb under the concrete overhang of a Burger King, watching the rain. Watching clean people with shopping bags, warm boots, and umbrellas jog by. Ghost and I are wet, our sneakers waterlogged, our clothes damp and stained.

A group of boys saunters by. One boy with a red cap whistles at Ghost and elbows his friend. "Look at the crack monkey!"

Ghost just sits there, smoking her cigarette, looking at the nice ladies holding shiny things and umbrellas. So many bags filled with nice things. They are all in a rush. I know that Ghost is hungry, desperate for one of the nice ladies to take notice of her like one of their possessions, to take her home and fix her up. Some of the ladies already have daughters. Pretty blond ones with clean clothes and white teeth. They live in bright bedrooms with white comforters and always get their schoolwork done on time.

The concrete overhang at the Burger King's entrance is wide enough to protect the top of your head from the rain, so Ghost and I shelter under it as the rain pours. A middle-aged woman with curly hair sits down next to us and passes us a pamphlet, searching Ghost's eyes.

"If you need food, a place to sleep ..." the woman says.

"I'm okay. I don't need anything," Ghost says, her chin in her chest.

"Keep that. Do you want a little something to eat? We have sandwiches."

"No. I have a home. I just want to stay here."

The concrete begins to melt in the spitting rain, and the woman disappears. Ghost is balancing a new unlit smoke between her middle and index fingers, her once youthful skin worn and patchy.

CHAPTER 13

The Invitation

WHEN THE INVITATION TO ATTEND CONVOCATION at the university comes, Mama, filled with pride, books a small room in a hotel across from the tourist attractions on the Inner Harbour.

On the ferry to the Island, we stand on the deck, lean against the thick metal railing, and watch the waves crash against the side of the boat as the wind tangles our hair.

"Look"—Mama points to the water—"the sun in the waves."

And I let myself mentally sink into the deep, cool waters of the strait.

The Days Inn is a beige cement building with potent yellow and blue signs. Because it is summer, the walkways below are dotted with stands selling ice cream and art, and people with cameras, beige shorts, and small children shuffle down the concrete corridor. Tourists pause for family photos on the bridge, in front of the water, or with the mime.

Mama holds up the small plastic bottles of shampoo and conditioner in the bathroom and clicks her tongue appreciatively. She grazes her palm against the soft white robe in the closet and slides her feet into the complementary slippers.

"These are nice."

I fidget with my phone, tracing its grooves and sleek metal casing. "I'm going for a walk," I tell her.

Mama looks over and says something about high tea, and Ghost begins singing, her achy song swimming beneath my lungs. This ache, Ghost's ache, will swallow my entire chest. It freezes my heart, my breath, my jaw. At times, I try to curb her hunger. I feed her warm food, sit in scented baths, imagine a life with Jude somewhere quiet and sunny. These memories with Jude are my own. So I store them in whichever vessels are free. Sometimes, this works. Ghost will accept the moment of love and forget. Sometimes she stops wailing and soaks in the warmth with me, but only for a bit. Then she remembers she is trapped and unearths another memory.

The next morning Mama and I catch a taxi to the university. We arrive at the corner of the campus, near the bus loop. Mama holds her chin up, taking long strides that stretch out her legs, signalling to the other parents that she is on campus for good reason. We cross the street, our heels clipping the ground like an offbeat drum kit. All the buildings are taupe and beige, square and short. Ghost is tickling my chest, filling it with air until laughter erupts, because these beige buildings with tiny cracks do not remind me of books or of following the path to a career. Instead, they remind me of nights with Sam and the dizzy drinks that kissed my lips. Mama is up ahead, bursting with pride as we approach the theatre.

We pass a table with framed certificates, sweatshirts, water bottles set up on the walkway. "We should look," she says.

"A frame? It's a waste of money, I don't need one."

Ghost is remembering the dizzy drinks, lightly trailing her fingers up and down my neck and shaking my eyes until the world is spinning.

"You must have your certificate framed. Everyone gets them framed. Look, just like these." Mama points to the table, where a sleepy-eyed boy is in charge of framing students' certificates.

"Let's look after the ceremony," I tell her.

Mama smiles, and Ghost giggles. "And after, we should do high tea. I've always wanted to have tea here."

I think of Mama's math flash cards.

High Tea: Expensive
Graduation Certificate: Unaffordable
Graduation Certificate Frame: Expensive

⚘

Dozens of students, joined by proud parents and siblings, student volunteers, and professors, congregate around the entrance to the theatre, excitedly trading stories of their postgraduate lives so far. There is a small check-in table where we give our names and receive a room number for the small building next door where we will wait and line up, then we collect our caps and gowns.

Over in the small building, a woman with short hair and stud earrings calls out over the crowd: "All students, please follow the signs on the classroom doors. Your last name will determine which group you're in. If you have any questions, please ask me or Dr. McNielson."

I enter a room filled with students all excitedly catching up, their hands flapping and fanning. A girl with well-styled hair and a sheer blue blouse says she has been travelling. She flew over the waves to the bustling streets of Thailand, where she bonded with elephants and rejoiced on white sand beaches. Her friend with high cheekbones and a large brown belt did some volunteering and then worked on applications to the MA program. My heart—not Ghost's, but my own—aches, because I am envious. Because I am trapped.

Dr. McNielson prepares us to walk into the ceremony, gathering each of us small hens to the front of the room to wait in single file, our bodies hidden by the shiny blue gowns. I wait in line, shifting my weight from one side to the other, balancing in my kitten heels, breathing through the small aches that are beginning to sound around the balls of my feet.

The two girls are bursting with excitement, chests high, teeth exposed, and small sounds of pleasures bubble up from their throats as we begin walking down the hallway. Dr. McNielson leads our room from the front. Ahead of us is another line of students in shiny blue smocks. Ghost is anxious now. Her legs are stretching out, pushing against my belly, extending the soft parts of my skin and trapping air as she takes up space.

This is not my place, I think to myself, and Ghost agrees. We walk past classrooms with warm orange doors and busy green chalkboards, down the hallway to the exit. Small blue hens shuffling past the squat trees to the theatre, whose seats are already filled by parents.

We stand side by side, eyes blinded by hot white lights, listening to speeches, waiting to hear our names and collect our paper certificates. Ghost reaches up into my throat to find my tongue and pushes down so I cannot speak. When she is scared, she stretches out until she fills all the crevices of this body; she makes herself large and fearless. I stand stock-still on the platform, my mouth stretched into a smile, my palms slamming into one another each time a name is called, each time a person skips to the front.

I am next, I think, my eyes squinting into the light, and Ghost whines until the lights are blinding me. I unearth a memory of Sam, her pale eyes and thick hands. The applause continues, and I step down onto the stage, my teeth bared as I swim into the light.

CHAPTER 14

The Hospital

ON THAT DAY IN NOVEMBER, the sun stretched itself across the sky before fading into the greasy blue of night. Ghost's movie of her hospital stay is wrapped up in my vessels, bundled, nestled beneath my tongue. Ghost, wrapped in a thin blue smock, is swaying under the fluorescent lights of the eighth floor. The boy is gone, the front desk is unstaffed, and the rooms are empty.

"I have to pee," Ghost whispers to the RN who is slowly guiding her down the hallway. Overhead, the lights flicker and dim until there is only scratched beige linoleum and square white tiles. She flops against the wall because it is sturdy, it can hold her. And as the dark swings in, as the floor tiles dance and vibrate, conversation between other RNs flows in and out like waves. In and out. In and out, before everything disappears.

CHAPTER 15

The Bath

AFTER THE GRADUATION CEREMONY, I leave the building, away from the other students and the camera flashes, away from Mama, who still sits proudly in her velvet seat. My back is tight, muscles frozen as I play with my phone and call Jude. Sweet Jude.

"I miss you," I blurt out as soon as they answer.

I can hear Jude's fingers flicking a thick piece of cardboard or drumming the edge of a table.

"I miss you too, how are you?"

"I'm all right. Just finished." More people are sweeping through the doorways, parents and children carrying certificates and flowers.

Snap, snap, snap, Jude's fingers beat.

"I haven't talked to you all day. It feels strange. How's the Island? Have you seen anyone? What's it like being back?" Jude's voice is a roller coaster, their tongue speeding up and pausing, then speeding again.

"I haven't spoken with anyone. Mama and I went straight to campus. I like it here, the trees are big."

I am lying. There are brick buildings, there is a concrete walkway, there are patches of grass and a quiet roadway.

The students and their families continue filtering out of the theatre, filling the walkway and blocking my view of the entrance. Even though it is summer, the sky is a creamy grey, and a light drizzle has begun. I want to tell Jude that already this island is strangling me. That I need the city's lights and constant motion.

"Sounds nice," Jude says.

"On the ferry, Mama and I watched the waves, and it reminded me of your stories about Italy."

"Mm-hmm."

"The ceremony was long. I have to find Mama. I left her inside. She wants to have high tea."

"High tea sounds fancy. Will you dress up?"

"I may just go back to the hotel. I'm already tired."

"It'll be fun," Jude says, and the *snap, snap, snap* of their fingers slows down as I laugh.

"Sleeping?"

"Do you think you'll see him, since you're on the Island?" Jude's voice is faraway, muffled as though coming from beneath the thick surface of an ice rink.

"See who?"

I see Mama standing across the way, where families are celebrating, her hand gripping the paper program. She is smiling to herself.

"Do you plan to see him?"

"I don't have any plans to see anyone."

"I hope you'll tell me if you do see him."

"Of course."

I grip my palm, dig my nails into the flesh.

"I should go."

Ghost is kicking my heart.

"I'm sorry I couldn't make your graduation. I would have come if I didn't have to work," Jude says.

"I know. It's weird. I don't even want to be here."

Ghost's tiny pointed toes dig into the softest part of my chest.

"If you do see him, I hope you'll tell me."

"I will."

"I'll try to call you around two o'clock." Jude's voice is muffled again.

Snap, snap, snap.

Back at the hotel, in the bathroom, I remind myself in Jude's voice that I am a miracle. The bathroom smells like vanilla and is the colour of a giant stain, an off-white, yellowing bruise. The warm glow of the bulbs accents the heat of the bathroom.

I tear off my dress and look at the person in the mirror. I study her long hair and the tiny dark pockmarks sprinkled over her nose. The tattoos that cover her shoulders and arms: butterflies, black widows, flowers. I sweep my eyes over her curved hips and the fine hairs on her tummy. I look her in the face and gaze into her eyes. Hazel eyes, deep brown with small flecks of gold.

I look at her until I feel the weight of myself humming through this body, slipping into the hollowed spaces. My body.

"I love you," I whisper, as my pupils dilate.

Ghost slithers up past my belly, over my ribcage, along my throat, until her voice is audible.

"I don't love you," she hisses, her voice engulfing my body before she slithers back down. The words dance across my chest and find a home beneath my scalp, curtained by strands of hair.

"I don't love you."

Her memo, her reminder, as she slides past my stomach and deep into my bones, into the marrow, which makes blood and feeds other animals, gives life. This is where she sleeps.

I can hear Mama. She is in the bedroom. I know she is unzipping her suitcase and pulling out her clothes. Hanging the important items, the ones that are satiny, the colour of bursting hearts, or studded with shiny sequins.

"Are you busy?" she calls through the bathroom door.

I pretend not to hear her and turn on the water to draw a bath. I ignore the soft kitten taps on the door.

"I'm going to go look at the souvenir stands by the harbour. Would you like to come with me?"

The perfect bathwater is not too hot and not too cold. My hand dips beneath the faucet's waterfall as I adjust the temperature.

"We can see if there's a waiting list for tea."

*

My first bath is at the boy's house. The doctors have instructed him to bathe me every day, to feed me, to give me three white pills every few hours.

He sits on the edge of the tub, holding his hand in the stream of water as he adjusts the taps.

"Not too hot, just in case. You have to be careful," he warns.

"Just in case," I repeat.

Above the bathtub, the stained-glass window shimmers. Light pulsates through the reds and blues, fading into a different rhythm than the loud rumble of water. I stumble backward, away from the lights and the noise, until all I can hear is Ghost's wailing.

I fall back into the dark, away from the crashing sea, deep into the heart of the boy's house. The living room with the cracked leather sofa that bleeds soft white foam and the small grey cat who sings like my Ghost. The crashing water is muffled from here, so the only noise is Ghost's wail.

The boy comes and leads me back to the bathroom, grabbing a towel from under the sink. The room is full of yellow light. Blue light. Red light.

"Almost ready," he calls, his voice bouncing off the walls and finding home in these ears. My ears. His lips speed over his words, gliding over each syllable quickly.

I stare at his chest, at the fabric binder noticeable beneath his thin baseball shirt. "I want to do this alone," I sputter, small beads of saliva bouncing into the air due to my heavy tongue.

The boy sighs. "I know, but I have to watch you. The doctor says we have to do this together."

"No, I'm doing it myself. Go away."

The boy slumps down on the toilet seat and puts his head in his hands. His fingers rub his forehead, press into his temples, squeeze the bridge of his nose.

"Alone," I repeat, my loud voice breaking.

"Listen, I'm going to help you into the bathtub first. You can take a bath alone, but I'm going to leave the door wide open, okay?"

He helps me take off my shirt, his hands swiftly pulling the fabric over my head. He invites me to put all of my weight on his shoulders as he bends down to take off my sweatpants.

I let him take my arm, I let him firmly squeeze my bicep and slip his other arm around my waist as though I were a small child.

"Easy, lift your left leg over the edge."

I listen to his words, chew and swallow them. I wait for each syllable to make its way into my brain, and then I tell my leg to lift.

Lift. Lift.

"No, the other leg." He laughs. "Now you have an excuse for your lack of direction."

I consume these words and allow them to sink into this brain. My brain.

"Now the other leg," the boy says.

I drop my foot into the bathtub, pushing against the water, and grip the boy's arm as he plops me down into a sitting position.

"I'm good," I tell him. He wipes his hands on the fluffy towel that is folded on the toilet seat.

"I'm leaving the door open," he reminds me.

I lean back against the curve of the eggshell-white bathtub, and the water heats my body. Washes away the hospital grime. I use my strong arm, the left one, to squeeze shampoo into my right palm and slather it onto my scalp. The right-hand side of my body is still numb and letting off electrical sparks; that arm is weak. I wash my hair with my left arm. I wash my body the same way. When I am finished, I do not call for the boy, I do not call for his help. Instead, I swing my arms over the edge of the tub and crawl out.

I let the water come with me. I push waves onto the tiled floor, over the bath mat, and crawl to Ghost's bedroom, leaving a trail of water in the hallway. Dry off my body on her bedsheets, beneath her blankets. She is still crying, wailing, punching her fists against my temples. She does not want me to clean myself; she does not want me to lose her scent.

⚘

The hotel bathtub is wide, and even after I turn off the taps, small drips of water escape from the faucet. The water is warm; it heats my skin, my blood. Ghost sighs in relief because the water reminds her of the suburban sun. And I sigh because the scent of vanilla reminds me of life, and I think of sweet, sweet Jude, whom I will marry by the water, surrounded by beetles and rich greenery.

CHAPTER 16

The Boy's House

A YEAR AFTER THAT DAY IN NOVEMBER, the boy left his apartment in the city for a crooked farmhouse built near the peak of a mountain. He says that living away from the bustle of the city, next to quiet waterways and dark earth, feels better for him. The crooked farmhouse is deep in the woods, surrounded by pine trees and swollen clouds, near the thin road's bend and the community mailbox. He now has a sad-eyed dog named Murphy and can finally grow facial hair that catches threads of light and the small particles of the seasons.

The boy says that when he first moved into this farmhouse, the old porch, which is stained with age and softened by the weight of rain, could barely hold him. So he found planks of thicker, more suitable wood and built a new, stronger porch. He tells me that in the early morning hours, he bundles up and slips outside to watch the long grasses bending in the northern winds and the mountains looming in the distance.

We sit in folding chairs on his new porch and look at the mountains together. I picture other homes far away, beneath the clouds, with people sitting on their balconies, looking across the way toward the boy's house. After we've spent time quietly drinking in the view, the boy turns to me, his eyes wide, as if this is the first time we've met.

"Your hair is long now. You look so different," he says lightly, and I shrug, smile at the snowy mountains.

"Your view is incredible."

He leans forward, resting his forearms on his knees. His gaze meets mine.

"Do you remember anything?" he asks.

I want to play him one of my silent films. See, this is when Ghost topples headfirst into the glass jar, and the world shifts. There is a river filled with pebbles that bounce, obstruct the view, and the jar is floating, floating, floating. And the world is moving, so quickly, while outside, locusts collide with the jar, buzzing in different pitches. I want to show the boy that there are some memories ingrained in this body. To tell him that somewhere deep down, she is still alive. But instead I look away, at the sprawling mountains, the bending grass.

"I tried snowshoeing last year," I tell him. "There are these tiny little birds that'll land in the palm of your hand if you hold out seeds. Isn't that incredible?"

"Whisky jacks. Those little birds are called whisky jacks," he mumbles, taking a sip of beer.

I play with a hangnail on my finger, carefully tearing it until dots of glossy red spring to the surface of my skin. The boy balances his bottle on his knee.

"I can tell you what I remember," he offers, and I meet his gaze, while the world holds its breath for a second time.

Ghost stirs, her lips glaze over mine, and she says, "Tell me."

The boy takes another sip of beer.

"You came home after class. Then we went right out again, grocery shopping. I had so many things to grab from the store, such a long list."

"It was dark?"

"I don't know, probably. You kept saying you weren't feeling well, and you were dragging your feet all over the store. Jesus, I thought you were just being dramatic, I didn't know there was actually something wrong. I mean, you always thought there was something serious going on just when you had a cold or something. Remember that one time we went out for dinner and you started getting stomach cramps? You had me to take you to the hospital, and it was only gas." He is smiling as these words spill over his lips.

He takes another sip, eyes focusing on something beyond me.

"I didn't know that you were, you know. Shit. You told me that you were sick." His voice shakes and slips beneath the surface until it is neither present nor gone.

My eyes settle on a small white bubble of paint on the deck. They trace over the clump as Ghost's fists wrap around my heart.

"I didn't know," the boy says again. "Remember the drunk lady? She was so annoying. They had to kick her out. I was losing my shit."

"In the hospital?"

"Yeah. That whole family was drunk because someone was dying."

"No, she was by herself, I remember. I heard her right outside my room. You and Mama were scared and the RNs chased her away because she was trying to hurt me."

"That isn't what happened ..." the boy says.

But Ghost is dreaming again. She has my hand, and we are walking through the tall grass in the boy's front yard, through the lush trees, over the rivers and roads, past shiny cars, all the way across the giant ocean and back to the hospital.

CHAPTER 17

The Dark

ON THE EIGHTH FLOOR OF THE HOSPITAL lives a witch. At night, as Ghost stares up at the stained ceiling tiles with tiny black holes that dance from left to right, the witch's cackle streams down the halls. This warning is hidden beneath my right breast; a thick brown mole marks this reminder, keeps my body safe.

Ghost taps the nerve of my tooth.

Tap, tap, tap.

The faded postcards of her stay in the hospital show her frail body on display, hospital gown riding over her panties.

Tap, tap, tap.

In the evenings, the boy must leave the hospital.

"I want to go too," Ghost whines, as he stands from his chair and zips up his jacket.

"Pull your blanket up, you're showing everyone your box," the boy says.

And in response, Ghost giggles.

❦

When Ghost shows me the darkened hospital, she becomes confused, for the darkness also reminds her of the park by her home in the suburbs. So Ghost shows me the hospital machines, blankets, and her tiny legs sprawled at an awkward angle, then we watch the dark spill over everything like thick molasses, heavy and stifling, until it reaches our toes, and we fall into the sweetened mess.

When I open my eyes, I am on a blanket of dewy grass and warm dark. My lips are sticky with apple cider and someone else's lips: a girl wearing black lipstick. We are hidden in the carefully curated leaves of the park's shrubbery. Surrounded by excited laughter and the smell of fire.

"Run!" a boy wearing a long sweater calls out to us.

My palms are pressed into the dirt, my lips pressed into the girl's.

Dizzy, we stand, gripping each other's hands, sweat beading against our palms as we run after our friends.

"Captain set the toilet paper on fire and the alarm went off!" The long-sweatered boy is choking back laughter.

The fire alarm fades behind the pounding of our sneakers. The girl has let your hand loose and slipped over to another girl with short, dark hair and ivory skin. The night, heavy with dew, drips over our bodies and buries us.

"Do you remember?" Ghost whines, and she slips her memory like a love note beneath one of my muscles. "This was so long ago." She slides her veins over the muscle, to ensure this moment will not be lost.

And while this is happening, busy Ghost buries *this* memory, from this moment in time, as well.

❦

During the day, while the moon and the witch are sleeping, after the boy returns to the hospital, Ghost is the star of the sideshow. A tall man in a lab jacket with pearly teeth and crisp eyes visits her, tells her she is in good hands.

The boy sits in a faded blue chair, his thin frame supported by the chair's plastic arm, and Mama looks out the dusty window at the trees whose red leaves whisper and flap against each other, branches swaying. It is morning now, and the sun touches all of the tables and chairs until they are golden, glowing from its heat. Ghost and her mama are holding hands. Mama's hands are delicate, tiny nude birds.

Ghost is hidden beneath the blankets, beneath her gown, beneath the sunlight, beneath her mama's hands.

"Mama?"

"Yes?"

"Do you remember yesterday, when we were sitting in the grass?"

"Mm-hmm."

"I was wearing pink shorts and that shirt with the bear on it. You were sitting with the other parents on the grassy hill and I was down near the tire swings."

"Oh yes, I remember."

"I was playing with a girl and I got hurt—I lost my entire toenail."

"Yes, I remember."

"Mama? It wasn't her fault. I wasn't wearing shoes, and my toes were bare. Do you remember?"

"Yes, yes."

"That girl I was playing with, she was nice. She was the only one who would push me on the swing."

"Oh yes."

"She shared the tire swing with me, and when I fell, I ripped my toenail off. I did it. It was me. It wasn't her. I couldn't tell anyone at the time because I was crying, but it wasn't her fault, she was good, she was just pushing the swing."

"It's okay."

"The girl with the pretty hair."

And then the room fades, and Ghost's blankets are loose again, and an RN is kneeling beside her bed.

"Do you know what day it is?"

Ghost giggles.

"No. I can't tell. It's always the same day here."

"Her surgery is tomorrow," the RN tells the boy and Mama.

The boy's face turns sour. "She's getting worse. We've already been waiting for days," he says, his voice slamming into the walls and the window that looks out on the forest of red trees.

"My head hurts. Can I have more pain stoppers? My head hurts," Ghost calls over to him.

CHAPTER 18

Oranges, Mustiness, and Nicotine

WE ARE STATUES ON THE BOY'S PORCH as the sun begins to dip its round belly behind the mountains.

"Is it almost five o'clock?" I am asking the mountains, I am asking the pine trees.

"Yeah, I can give you a ride back to the hotel, if you like." He is telling the ashtray, he is telling his knee.

"I'm sorry," I whisper, as we both float toward the clouds. A dog is barking from somewhere below.

"For what?" he asks.

"Just ... everything."

Ghost stirs. Her legs are stretching, pushing against my ribs, my sternum, her ballerina toes curling around the softest parts of my throat until she has filled every fissure. With one swift kick, she knocks my chin hard, again, again, until my lower lip quivers beneath her weight.

"I feel better now," I lie, allowing the mountains to sharpen into focus.

"I know it was difficult for you as well, your poor brain." He clears his throat, swings his hand over his knee, and pats down, his fingers drumming along to a secret tune. "Can I ask you something?" he says, his fingers pausing for a second. "Do you remember anything?"

Ghost lands one final kick and pauses, allows a stream of air to slip into my lungs, allows some space for his words to trickle down.

"Everything before I woke up is like one long dream. Some pieces are missing or disconnected. Sometimes I can't connect the parts, or the way I remember things is different."

"Makes sense."

"I like when you tell me stories. It helps." And Ghost nods, because she likes this as well.

"Yeah, well, my memory is shit, especially during that time, so I don't know how much help I can be," the boy says, laughing, and Ghost tickles my heart until I smile as well.

"You have such a stunning view. Congratulations on your place," I whisper, as Ghost begins to wail again.

"Yeah, thanks."

"Is it beautiful at night?"

"You know what I remember the most?" the boy says to the trees in the distance.

"No."

"Your laugh."

"I don't laugh the same anymore?"

"I wouldn't know," he says.

I'm unsure of what to say, so we sit in silence, and as he mourns her, I fall into the teal-blue mountains and listen to the wind. I wait for him to say something else, to end this uncomfortable wake, but he is still, so we listen to the dog barking and the wind and Ghost's wails.

And now we are different statues on his porch, and the sun has spread herself across the sky, until all that remains are wispy streaks of pink.

"We should probably go now," he tells the mountains, he tells the pine trees.

*

The boy's truck is familiar. It smells of oranges, mustiness, and nicotine. The seats are thick and well padded, built for those who drive for long hours.

"You have the address? My phone is a bloody piece of shit, can't connect it to my truck." He laughs.

"It's right by the Inner Harbour, just across the street."

"Oh fancy," he says, as his truck growls to life and lurches forward. Then it speeds over the roads until the homes blur, the people blur, and the trees leave small traces of themselves behind, staining the image. A furious mesh of colour and movement. And meanwhile, I am sitting in his passenger seat, the same seat Ghost once did, but everything is different now, even though it seems strange that time has passed.

"I graduated. That's why I'm here on the Island."

"I know, you told me already."

*

On the drive back from the hospital, I sit in his truck. The once familiar scent of oranges dressed in smoke is now hidden under a metallic taste whose sharp edges cut into my nostrils, stinging the edge of my tongue.

"It smells," I whisper.

"Yeah, that's you!" The boy laughs. "We could smell you when they were wheeling you down the hall! I had no idea what it was. Even your mom ..." The boy stops talking, and the trees swim by.

"Why do I smell like this?"

The boy rolls down the window, and fresh air blasts into the truck.

"I think it's from the surgery, I don't know. They put glue in you."

I try to remember what I'm supposed to smell like, but I can't. I can only taste something strong and tangy. It's attached to the air inside of me.

"Glue?"

"Yeah, I don't really understand what they did, but that's what the doctors said, something about glue."

"They put glue in me?"

"I don't really get it," he says again.

"Why?"

"I don't know. It helps your brain. Something about the vessels. It's bloody weird."

The boy airs his truck out until his familiar scent returns, and after time, my new smell settles in. It seeps into my skin until it is a part of me. Even the boy becomes used to it, so much so that he claims it is beginning to fade.

Whenever the boy tells people about the hospital, he stands at an invisible microphone, a cigarette crunched between his fingers. When the boy's stepfather visits the apartment, he takes a seat, listens with glee as the boy performs. His stepfather, wide eyed and smirking, nods, leans forward as the boy weaves him in.

"I was sitting in the waiting room. It was getting so late."

"Mm-hmm."

"And then the nurses finally come around and tell me that she's all right. So me and her mom go and stand at the end of the hallway to wait for her."

The boy's stepfather has cracked a beer, his eyes still on the boy.

"So, we're waiting, and then all of a sudden, the elevator door opens, and before I even know if it's her, I smell this odour!"

Stepfather is snorting, Stepfather is struggling to swallow.

"What do you mean?"

The boy taps his knee. "She reeked like burnt glue! I could smell her before I saw her!" he says.

The boy and his stepfather are giddy. The boy looks at me and winks.

"Oh! When she gets mad, tell her not to get unglued!" the boy's stepfather adds and takes another sip. Another sip. Another sip.

I am watching from my chair. Ghost is not pleased; she has slouched down, somewhere hidden, somewhere safe.

"Yeah, yeah, I'll be sure to use that one," the boy says with a smirk.

"Funny, huh? Unglued?" Stepfather shakes his head.

My lips shakily lift to display a row of teeth.

"Funny," I repeat.

⚘

But now, the boy's truck smells of him, and Ghost enjoys the scent, because it is a vessel to where she belongs. She squeezes my heart and swims in each flavour, licks the musty oranges, reaches for another story, begins unearthing her unfinished dreams.

"You can drop me off before the hotel," I offer.

"Okay, I'll let you off here," the boy says, and he pulls over beside a statue of a man and a little girl and a real family taking photographs and eating ice cream.

"Thank you for the ride," I say and step out onto the pavement. Ghost continues digging, her fingers looping around each story, stitching pieces from the boy's home, the warm spot on the sofa, his oceanic bedroom, his smell.

She is lost in visions of the boy's truck rumbling down the street, over the pavement, past the tall buildings and furry trees and all the subdued colours against the faded sky. She can still only smell her new scent.

His truck passes over the small concrete bridge and into the touristy part of the city. Dusk takes over, and all the statues and tourists eating ice cream are doused in gold.

CHAPTER 19

Jude and the Beach

"DID YOU AND YOUR MOM HAVE HIGH TEA?" Jude asks. I set my coffee on the table, place my hands around the mug for warmth. Mornings are always cold for me, even in the summer.

"We didn't have time."

Jude's eyes churn, their gaze washing over mine. "Why not?"

I think back to last week, to the crooked farmhouse near the peak of a mountain, the small blue hens and the convocation. I shrug my shoulders as Ghost pushes herself against my chest.

Ghost doesn't like it when Jude asks questions; she thinks they are nosy. When the questions begin, she drags her nails beneath my cheeks until they burn, bangs her fists against my ribs until they bruise, squeezes my windpipe until I am breathless.

"I was visiting someone," I whisper.

"So you did see him," Jude says, their chin pointing toward my chest, their lips chewing on thoughts that I do not want them to say out loud.

And Ghost squirms, because the boy is none of Jude's business.

"Yes, briefly."

Jude nods. "You were supposed to tell me if you saw him."

Ghost grips my heart, then releases slowly. The coffee mug is already cooling. The sun has pushed into Jude's home, spreading her warmth across the table and washing it over the tufted grey carpet.

"I'm telling you now. I thought it would help. I still have questions."

Ghost has questions.

"Did you find out what you were looking for?"

"Not really."

"Why did you think he had answers?"

"He was there."

"It doesn't make sense. What would he know that you and your mom don't?"

"I don't remember things. My mom wasn't always there."

"Did seeing him help?"

"Not really. He said he didn't remember."

"None of this makes sense."

I look toward the window, watch the clouds wash over the sky. Ghost has stopped singing; she has worn herself out. She is asleep again, drowning in her own world, privately. Her wails have stopped and my chest is empty, filling with air. Everything is quiet. When she is tired, removed, the world is still. All I taste are my thoughts, my desires. Everything is my own. Quietly, securely my own.

Across the table sits my Jude, with their smoky eyes and their crooked nose. My Jude, whose mouth is a curved moon. Their lips, thick and pink, etched with a thin grey line. A scar from another fight.

"I love your lips," I tell Jude, and they force a smile.

"Portuguese," they respond.

And I remember what Jude has told me before, that their lips are a gift from a long line of relatives who lived and died in the farm fields. They get their lips from a grandfather. I have seen the photos.

I remember. Jude's grandfather is short. He is stalky. He has a plump nose and a big smile.

"Tell me again," I say, "about your grandparents."

Because now, without Ghost, we can discuss something besides the boy. Now we can fill our minds and lips with our own discussions.

Jude shakes their head, looks down at their coffee mug, and mumbles, "My mom told me he worked in the field every day, every day until he could no longer move. He was a farmer, so he had to start early. And every morning, my grandmother woke long before him to make his breakfast."

"What did she make him?" My hand finds home on Jude's knee.

"Two slices of toast, because bread was cheap and filling. They had to make do with whatever was available. So it was always bread. Flour was inexpensive."

I know that Jude loves this story; they usually tell it as a prelude to our life dreams. A swollen hope that we will find a place in line with our ancestors, who were fighters. A long line of fighters.

"You make bread," I say.

"Mm-hmm. They worked all day, every day. On good days, there were bits of cheese and eggs. That was life."

"My great-grandfather worked in the fields as well."

"Tell me again," Jude says, their other hand gently covering mine. A peace offering.

"He owned a farm in the Punjab, but the Brits chased him off the land when he refused to pay their taxes."

Ghost's Mama told me this story a few months ago as we were sifting through her father's items, gently laying each artifact of his life down on the carpeted floor. She held up yellowed photographs and trickled out hearsay and dollops of information.

"This was a long time ago," Mama said, pointing at a man in his fifties with a long beard in a turban and a suit. "This is your great-grandfather, Naranjan. He was so kind. He taught me how to read."

Mama's story is shades of yellow and grey, just like the photograph. Mama, sitting on her grandfather's lap, laughing, flipping through her picture book. Naranjan looks proud, his nose shiny in the glow of the living room lamp.

"After we get married, I'd like to go fishing in the same waters as my ancestors."

"In Portugal?"

"Yes."

"Do you think your grandparents were in love?"

"I don't know. Yes. Working together was a necessity. They didn't have other options." Jude's lips purse, and a soft grey clouds their eyes. "My grandparents did love each other. I remember."

In the distance, a siren calls.

"Jude?"

"Yes?"

"I want to go to Italy with you. I want to lie on the sand by the water. I want to go to the secret beach you told me about when we first met."

I imagine my skin glowing beneath the sun's rays, my hair bleached the same colour as the faded grains of the sand. Still, when I think of Italy, a memory of my old rain-soaked ceiling follows. When I picture the golden dunes and imagine how my sticky, salty skin will feel pressed against Jude's frame, I also feel the itchy carpet of my apartment and smell the musty odour left by the previous tenants.

"We'll go to Italy first," Jude promises, their finger tracing over an imaginary ring on my left hand.

I like this idea, because it is somewhere Jude and I can begin afresh. Italy is a place untouched by Ghost. Italy flourishes only in my own dreams.

"But I'd also like to go to the beach with you today." Jude smiles.

"I'd like that."

"Let's try for this afternoon."

And the sun touches Jude's face, kisses their lips, their scar.

"I'd like that," I say again, and join the sun.

❧

In Seattle, there is special beach for queers on the shore of Lake Washington. For us. It is removed from the larger beach, just a small patch of sand surrounded by a low concrete wall for privacy. This beach is a reminder of the dream Jude and I share. One day, back in March, after the grass had thawed and the leaves were beginning to grow, Jude traced their promises and hopes all along my left index finger, over one of Ghost's tales. We decided that our private union should take place someplace by the ocean, among fir trees. Jude says that grounding ourselves in nature is important. I could see the sturdy trees, feel the cool water dragging across my naked toes, numbing them in its icy grip. Being in the water reminds me that I am alive, that I am present.

At the beach for queers, Jude and I find a spot near the edge of the water. Across the way, a stereo is spilling out a sea of pop music. Tiny grains of beach dust jump across our towels as we spread them out on the sand.

"This is perfection," I say, pulling off my shorts and T-shirt and sitting down on my towel.

Jude smiles and removes their ribbed tank top. "Will you get my back?"

They pass me the sunscreen and face the water, their back almost fully exposed. Their chest is only hidden by a sports bra. I massage the thick cream onto their back, taking care to rub in the streaks of bright white until they disappear. Then I do the same across the visible portion of their chest. Over the tattoo that is important for family reasons.

"You never miss a spot," Jude says with a sigh.

"I can't let you burn. I like you far too much, and I want to spend time with you after the beach."

"After the beach? Maybe. I might be sick of you by then." They smile, eyes closed.

"Will you still feed me?"

"Probably not."

"But then I'll starve."

"You might. Bye-bye, birdie."

"I should just let you burn, then." I gently slap Jude's shoulder and reach behind them for the small cooler we packed that morning. Inside, there are tiny sandwiches and fresh berries in small plastic containers lined with folded paper towel to capture the bread crumbs and the rich juices.

When the sun is at its highest point, with our bellies full from the sandwiches and berries, we waddle down to the water. Jude hops along a self-made path and thrashes through the icy ripples, their stocky arms bracing to dive. The wind holds its breath, allows the sun to heat my body a little more as I tenderly dip my toes in, wait to get used to the temperature change.

"Come in, it's so warm!" Jude purrs from the water.

Timidly, I step in farther, allowing the water to swish around my ankles and lick at my calves.

"It's too cold!" I squeal.

"Just jump in! It'll only be cold for a second."

I fill my lungs with warm air and then plunge in face first, my eyes squeezed shut. My nerves pop as the water swallows my body, freezes me.

"Your body will get used to it, just swim around a bit. The water is perfect now," Jude says.

My legs are already kicking furiously, cutting through the undertow, pushing against the water's grasp. My head slips beneath the waves—two, three, four—and then breaks the surface—two, three, four.

Ghost remembers this. Fresh water is familiar to her. Cool, blue, freeing.

"Let's swim to the dock," Jude calls, bobbing gently in the waves. The water's earthy aroma is a distant memory, a dream I once had, where the world was softly fading.

My legs kick feverishly as I swim farther and farther from Jude. They are yelling something, but all I can hear is the loud slaps of crashing water.

Fir trees like tiny green hats decorate the other side of the lake. Jude has disappeared, and I am alone. Just me and the tiny trees and the calm lake and the distant, excited calls of other people. As I float on my back, the water rumbles through my ears and over my body, suffocating Ghost's cries. I flip onto my stomach, reach my arms forward, curve my elbows, and create an *S* shape, start cutting through the water at an angle, because Ghost's body still understands how to swim. It still remembers.

And the water, the water is important. So Jude and I will hold hands and trade promises on the beach in the heavy sea air beneath flocks of seagulls, far, far away from the Island, far away from the boy and all of Ghost's stories.

CHAPTER 20

Ghost's Song

GHOST SINGS TO ME OF HER TRAVELS, songs about Philadelphia and art school. She wants me to know that once upon a time, she was free. Most of these are sung in bent chords that smash against my teeth, salty lyrics about jewelled women ripe with love and autumn leaves as frayed confetti for her farewell celebration. She shows me the SEPTA station at Locust and Walnut, where we sit on the subway seats, thighs damp under summer's ragged tongue. And the brick-walled pub with cheap shots and tall cans, where she pressed her lips like a handshake by the pinball machine and danced against the back-alley walls. Later, she'd find solace on her bathroom floor, the ancient linoleum, stretched out beneath another's arm as he sucked her breasts. Here, she was free, and the many hands that held her did so gently, even if they were rough.

And the tale of Meredith, which Ghost has carved into my right thumbnail, because this one is important to her. She tells me that Meredith lived in a row house in South Philly, across the street from a barber shop and ten minutes from the SEPTA station. The row house is where Ghost lay beside Meredith and let her smooth out Ghost's heartbeat with her touch. Small breasts, short breaths.

So when Ghost phoned Meredith and asked her for another date, the response seemed jagged and cold. It slithered out in rash whispers, slapping Ghost's earlobes, eardrums, until her lips trembled beneath the weight of disappointment, of lost lust. And then Ghost's eyes met my own before she dragged me back into another song. And this is where Ghost says that Meredith revealed there was another woman waiting for her. One with an hourglass figure who worked in fashion, one who Meredith was ready to move in with.

The night before Ghost died, she and the boy drove to Walmart. Ghost's memory of this night is loosely woven into the slippery threads of my left lymph node. There is a dark parking lot where yellow street lamps illuminate a red car, blue car, silver car.

Wrapped in her blue jacket and mittens, Ghost stumbles past the colourful cars into the faded store. The boy is up ahead, rushing from aisle to aisle, collecting things for their home—cleaning spray, dish towels, soap.

Ghost tells me that usually, when she and the boy go to Walmart, she pretends she can buy whatever she wants from the store. She stands in front of the mirror, holding blouses against her body, slipping her fingers over their thin, satiny material, wishing she could try them on.

But tonight Ghost is tired, as if she has had too many dizzy drinks, so she drags her feet, refuses to lift them. She shuffles into the women's clothing section, amid the round silver racks blossoming with bright clothes. The lights are dim, and shoppers are murmuring, their voices muffled as though behind the veil of another world.

The boy bustles down the aisle, pushing a cart filled with boxes.

"If you're so tired, why did you come?" The boy is tired as well.

Ghost shrugs and struggles to lift her chin. "I'm sick."

He sighs. "You just need sleep."

"I think I need to go to the hospital," she mumbles.

"You're just tired. I'll take you tomorrow before work if you still feel sick, okay?"

And Ghost shuffles behind him. As the boy pushes the cart toward the cash registers, Ghost sucks me deeper and deeper into her world. The lights are bright now, flashing like a moving subway car, and she flops like a rag doll. The floor shifts from beige to white, and the people in royal-blue vests who talk quickly start to blur. And as the store is fading, Ghost is travelling on the SEPTA, through the brick-lined tunnels, picking up different scents as she is flown from one station to the next. Outside the store, darkness swallows the red, silver, blue cars, and the street lamps disappear.

CHAPTER 21

The Feather Earrings

Part I

JUDE AND I HAVE TRADITIONS. I appreciate the calmness of our routine, the gentleness of our connection. On the second Friday of the month, I slip some clothes and makeup into my backpack and board the Greyhound bus from the casino in Richmond. We drive to the US border and cross over, then drive to downtown Seattle. I walk along Pine Street and across the bridge into Capitol Hill. Past the coffee shops and small boutiques, on my way to meet Jude. In the summer months, we take evening strolls past the grey treatment centre and the city lights of Pine Street. We stop at the ice cream shop and go to the park, where we lie on our backs, watching excited dogs and young acrobats practising their routines. On Saturday afternoons, we lie in bed, arms tangled around one another, Jude's chest drowning in my hair, dreaming of a different life together, a different world, somewhere warm and safe—just this feeling.

In Capitol Hill, across the street from a record shop and right beside a bookstore, is our diner. On Sunday mornings, while Ghost is still drowsy, it is easy to promise Jude that being in Seattle, being with them, is home. Our tradition is to order baked buns with homemade jelly and two cups of dark roast with sweetened almond milk. Jude slices the buns, and I mix my coffee with a dash of honey and most of the milk. Even when the diner is busy with clanking dishes and voices over voices, even after Ghost awakes to begin her wailing ballad, I trust Jude's eyes and focus on their soft humming as they butter the buns and spread the jelly, because I need to maintain this tradition.

Our diner is on Tenth Avenue, beside the grassy green park and the ice cream shop. When our bellies are full, our lips sweet with the memory of brunch, we walk down East Pike Street. I link my arm through theirs, my cheeks glowing from the salty breeze. There is an art store with woodsy scenes displayed on easels and a shop that sells locally made bitters and chocolate body butter. But our first stop is always the thrift store, a gorgeous window display of mannequins wearing fluorescent minidresses and cropped shirts. Our treasured thrift store, with records, books, and discarded hats craving attention. Along the back wall is a long glass case filled with precious pieces: crystal watches frozen in time, candy-bright jewellery—small studs with bronze backs, thick hoop rings, shiny plastic pieces that clip onto your earlobes. I dart my eyes from one jewel to the next, over shiny earrings and brooches, until I'm lost in the shimmer. Nestled atop the glass case is a silver stand sprouting more jewels.

Jude always saunters downstairs to the records section, hoping to uncover a treasure, to unearth something magnificent, while I float to the back of the store, to the jewels, the precious stones. Ghost enjoys this part of the store as well. We stare at the glamour, the bold ornaments, the rich magentas and marine blues. There are long, dangly necklaces and dainty feather earrings perhaps plucked from the band-tailed pigeons in Capitol Hill Park and then dyed the colour of syrup, the colour of amber. I study these closely and trail my fingers over the feathers.

Ghost likes them as well. She slides her fingers over my heart, curls around my neck, and sighs as I fondle the feathers. She wraps her hands around my own, and we tickle the tiny feathers over the sensitive lines on our palm, trace our lifeline. Ghost wraps her hands around the treasure and smoothly slips them into my jeans pocket.

Jude is downstairs sifting through a box of records, chin nodding to the beat of the music playing in the store. They already have five records snuggled under their arm.

"I found a few. I always find good ones here," they say with a smile.

Ghost's teeth are nibbling my ears, burning the cartilage.

"Are you almost ready to go?" I ask.

Jude is still flipping through albums, their face set in deep concentration.

"Yeah, sure. Did you find anything?"

"No."

My pocket is heavy, the feathers hot against my upper thigh, and Ghost is pushing her weight against my ribcage, leading me up the stairs toward the exit doors.

"You're almost there," Ghost whispers as the ground creaks, whisking me back into my body. I shove my hand into my pocket and whip the feather earrings out so they are in plain view. Sweating, I make my way to the front counter and the beautiful twink working the till. I place the feathers on the counter, cheeks burning.

"Do you need a bag?" the twink asks.

"No, I have pockets."

"It's two pairs of earrings for the price of one."

"I just want these," I mumble, as Jude comes up beside me.

"Almost lost you," they say, placing their records on the counter.

Because it is the weekend, Jude cooks while I have a bath. They tell me it's good for us to ground ourselves and be separate but in the same place. I leave Jude leaning over the oven and slip into the bathroom, the earrings gently cupped in my palm. Fragrant garlic and spices tickle my nose as I lather the silver, pointy bits of the earrings with soap, wash the feathers in Jude's yellow sink to Howlin' Wolf.

My hands are shaking as Ghost jabs a metal hook through the soft lobe of my ear.

"There, like that. These look so nice," I whisper.

Ghost squirms with delight as I admire the sleek pigeon feathers, noticing how they graze my shoulders. She guides my fingers through my hair, pulling it back from the left side of my face.

We are both mesmerized by the earrings.

"Yes. Just like that," I whisper. The mirror darkens, and the bathroom begins to throb. Sink, mirror, bathtub, tile. In the distance, the music sounds the reminder of another world as I slip into Ghost's.

"These are mine," she whispers, wiggling my Achilles heel. Sickly yellow flashes. The bathtub, the sink tilt, and the music throbs as my head crashes into the bathroom counter and I am swallowed by the night.

The Feather Earrings

Part II

🍃 UNDER THE MATTE-GREY SKY, a rusted blue truck winds down the road. Everything is soft in this image, untouched, and yet blended. There are trees with gold-tipped branches outside the truck as it bounces and crunches over the pebbled road. A brown-feather earring sits next to a pack of cigarettes in the cupholder. Ghost's body is hunched, doubled over in the passenger seat next to the boy.

The air is thick, silent, and warm, even though it's the dead of winter. Ghost's fingers grasp my wrist, pulling me deeper into her world, and we sink together, surrounded by her breath, engulfed in the night's arms. And Ghost, sneaky little thing, buries herself in the bundles of my muscles, ties them tight with veins and vessels.

🍃

It is still early when the boy wakes Ghost in bed. His hand falls lightly on her arm and shakes it like she is a small child, a precious doll.

"Let's go. Just grab your clothes. Let's be quick," he says.

He lifts her out of the bed to her feet. "Let's hurry," the boy whispers, and Ghost wobbles over to the dresser and pulls out a plaid button-up shirt and a pair of jeans.

Through the window, the sun burns the dark into a warm navy. Ghost wanders from her bedroom to the bathroom to the kitchen. She places herself in every room, haunts every nook and cranny, because they are hers.

"Let's go," the boy says again.

Outside, the seaside wind pushes strongly rooted plants over onto the sidewalk and swings the traffic light like a pendulum. The wind cuts through Ghost's jacket. She's hobbling, swaying with each strong gust.

Ghost and I sit in the passenger seat, her tiny head bobbing on each bump. The boy's truck flies past a coffee shop in a quiet neighbourhood with clean sidewalks and freshly mown lawns.

The boy helps Ghost from the truck to the clinic. He seats her in the waiting area beside two other women with grey hair and solemn faces.

"Wait here," he says to her and makes his way to the front counter.

Ghost sits, her chin lowered, pointing to the ground.

And the darkness, the place where I was born, hums.

The boy is in a rush, so the medical clerk lets us in early. She bustles us ahead of the other seated patients and leads us into the doctor's office. Ghost's head is still heavy, carrying the weight of the night.

A doctor with beautiful jewelled earrings enters the room.

"What seems to be the problem?" the doctor says to the boy, as she lifts Ghost's chin and peers into her eyes. Ghost focuses on the beautiful earrings, her lips quivering at the gleaming jewels.

"She said she was sick yesterday and I think ..." the boy's voice trails off.

"Do you notice her face?" the doctor says, placing her hand on Ghost's cheek and pulling downward.

"Yeah. It's drooping."

The porcelain-white papers on the doctor's desk are bursting with light. "So pretty," Ghost wants to tell the doctor, the boy, but her lips don't move here.

"It could be cerebral palsy. When did you notice her face?" the doctor asks the boy.

"Just this morning. We came right away."

"You should go to the ER," the doctor says.

And the boy nods. His expression is serious.

This day in November is Ghost's last day. As she draws her final moments, her hands clasp around my neck until I can taste her panic. Her pupils are enlarged, her short hair tangled in an unruly mop. She shows me how soft the world is now, how the edges of the furniture blur. The doctor with her glamourous red-carpet earrings fades, the boy and the office fizzle into nothing.

"So pretty," Ghost whispers, and the dark spits me out, back in the boy's apartment, back before the doctor's office, the previous morning, packing her bag for school. Warm lights and wooden floors. A silver coffee pot sizzles and lets out a gasp.

She picks up her Thermos and drags herself to the coffee maker. This takes a long time. Slowly and shakily, she pours the coffee.

The dark coffee splashes into her Thermos.

Everything is blurry.

Bound in a blue peacoat, she swims in and out of rooms, gathering her books and her phone.

The coffee is strong, acidic. It burns my mouth, curls my tongue as I sink deeper into Ghost. I am stumbling on the edge of reality, half in a dream. Let us place one foot in front of the other, keep our balance as we grasp the Thermos, our body swaying in a non-existent breeze. Ghost wobbles to and fro, a dizzy waltz from one side of the sidewalk to the other. The coffee scalds her esophagus. Instead of warm, comforting sweetness, the taste is too strong. After two small sips, she tosses the Thermos into her backpack. I do not enjoy her coffee, and maybe this is not unusual. I once heard that an overabundance of something can create distaste. The heavy clouds and soft world are nothing more than a side effect of too much. Too much.

Alone on the rain-slicked street, she does not pass cars or other people. The small children who sometimes play in the schoolyard, howling at the bell, have disappeared. The world is still as I settle into Ghost's body, lift one knee above the other, try to ground myself.

And you, Ghost, this is where you struggle to hide all of the important bits. The small threads of memory, your postcards. This is where you begin to bury them.

All that is left of that last day is cumulus clouds. A slight breeze rippling over the dark-hipped roofs of the neighbourhood. Ghost hobbling down the road. Great firs sway, and the large round buttons of her jacket wink in the fading sun. And then the dark flushes in. The light pulses, and Ghost's body grows heavy as the world softens.

Ghost and I will swim through the night, passing the cherry blossom clouds and the textures of her life. Here she is as a ballerina—her bony feet, her knobby knees. And here she is with the boy, her mouth ajar, her hands grabbing at his hair, her nails scratching down his back. We balance each memory beneath our tongue as we swim up toward the moon and watch the story of her death. This one is special, this one explains it all.

On that day in November, the boy and Ghost wait for centuries. The boy says there were many exams—CT scans, MRIS, angiograms, various blood tests—and Ghost agrees. Slumped in a wheelchair, she's taken from one room to the next, one exam to the next. Her fingers are sleeping birds resting comfortably on her thighs as her tiny head bumps from side to side. His own body swaying with exhaustion, the boy is drowned in worry as he pushes her from room to room, his hands gripping the wheelchair's handles.

Then, the hospital room with powder-blue sheets on the bed. Ghost and the boy wait in silence. Near silence. Ghost is still sniffling, swallowing the hospital air in quick breaths. The boy sits on a chair from across the gurney, his short dark hair slicked back, and scrolls through his phone.

"It is taking a long time," Ghost slurs.

"Yeah, it is taking a while." The boy pokes his head outside the curtain. "I'll be back, I'm going to try to find the doctor, okay?"

After a while he's back sitting in the chair again. He looks tired. He is missing work today, and Ghost is missing school. He plays with his phone some more and goes back out from time to time to smoke cigarettes and make telephone calls.

Every time the boy ruffles the curtains to exit the room, Ghost tells him "I love you." And each time he returns, she has forgotten that he left and so she says it again. "I love you."

Finally, a doctor with shiny, curly hair and an important-looking clipboard enters the room where Ghost and the boy are waiting.

"I have good news and bad news."

"Okay, give me the bad news," Ghost says.

"Well, I have to give you the good news first," the doctor says.

"Oh."

"The good news is, we know what's wrong. The bad news is ..."

And then everything goes black and Ghost is crying and the dark is suffocating us and the doctor looks concerned and then we're swimming in the night, breathing in the stars.

The doctor explains it all to the boy as Ghost's chest shakes with fear and tears stream down her face. This isn't right. Ghost is healthy. She quit drinking alcohol, quit smoking cigarettes, eats vegetables. She practises her breathing. She is young, this is a mistake.

"I want to go home," she whispers.

"We're going to send you to another hospital that is equipped with the proper devices and the right doctors to perform further testing." The doctor's face is healthy and clean. Her eyes are soft, and she seems uncomfortable. She is saying things that don't make sense. Her body glimmers beneath the yellow lights, and she begins to fade. We stare at her, distracted by hair engulfing her face. She is facing the boy now, telling him things. Ghost's head slumps forward, the tears begin again, and she sobs.

The doctor shifts. Her clipboard holds the answers.

"I want to go home," Ghost whispers to the boy.

"We have to go to another hospital," the boy replies.

"So pretty," Ghost whispers, as the world fades.

CHAPTER 23

The Feather Earrings

Part III

JUDE'S EYES ARE STAINED WITH WORRY, their lips pressed together, forming a puffy duck's beak. I know that my ankle is bruised. I can feel Ghost's fingers plucking my nerves, pinching my thin tendons until they tense. A familiar pain rides up my leg, along my back, and twists along my neck before settling into the roots of my teeth. Her hands busy with my ankle, Ghost's feet crowd my skull, kicking my temples to some unknown beat.

"I fell ..." I mumble, my head pounding as I lift myself off the linoleum.

"Careful, easy does it, are you all right?" Jude puts an arm around my shoulders.

"Yes, I slipped on the bath mat," I lie.

"You have to be careful," Jude says. Their strong hands gently ruffle through my hair, examining my skull for any sign of a bruise.

For the first time, I look closely at the bathroom floor. The linoleum is clean. There are no signs of dirt or debris, just age, which is ground so deep into the floor as to become part of it. The bathtub, rose pink with dark streaks from years of wear, gleams because Jude ensures that everything in their presence is well cared for.

"Mm-hmm, well, this isn't good," they mumble, their faded denim shirt close to my nose. Sometimes, more often than not, I want to curl up inside of them and live in their scent, in their stability.

"Am I bleeding?"

Jude's fingers are still playing with the same spot in my hair. Ghost's tiny feet are still kicking to an unheard tune.

"No. You have a bump, though."

"Really?" My fingers search my forehead, feel their way toward the pain.

"Professional opinion is, you'll have to be put down," they say with a sigh, a smile creeping over their face.

"Doctor, I need dinner first." My voice is shaky, my fingers still searching for a bump.

Jude's lips curl. "No, I'm afraid not. This is urgent."

"But I deserve dinner! I want my last meal!" I laugh. The murky visions of Ghost and her hellish story feel softer, smoother, in the presence of Jude's smoky eyes—a waterway without violent undertows or sea monsters.

"No time. Bye-bye, birdie." Jude kisses my forehead.

"I want Advil," I say, my hand still wrapped around Jude's arm, like Ghost but different because I am loving, not lusting. I care.

Jude moves to the small cabinet above the sink and grabs a small white pill bottle. "I like those earrings, they suit you," they say, handing me two pills. The feather earrings dance around my neck, tickle my shoulder as Ghost continues kicking, two, three, four.

Jude's scent is a musty memory of their Italian adventures—the beach, the Navy ship, the gelato, and the stories that are only their own. They have a small sample bottle of their amber-coloured cologne in the bathroom cabinet, next to the pain pills, above the stomach medication, below their hair products. When we move from the bathroom to the living room to the bedroom, their scent follows. Jude smells the way I want my home to smell. Like someplace sweet and distant, telling a story of a small fishing town surrounded by white sand beaches and deep-blue ocean. Jude's neck holds all of these memories not yet been sung.

"I love your smell," I mumble as I sink into the sheets, press my face against their chest, and listen to their breath.

"I want to move somewhere," I tell Jude.

"Where would you like to go?"

"Somewhere warm, like Italy or California or New York."

"New York isn't always warm, and I'm not interested in San Francisco anymore," they say.

"Anywhere. I what to live somewhere new with you. Somewhere that belongs to just us."

"Yeah? Well, rent is cheap in Portugal, and the water is clear. We can sit on the beach with fresh grapes and cheese." Their lips are puckering again. I picture their eyes shining in this dream.

"Tell me more," I say, nestling deeper into their chest.

CHAPTER 24

Ghost's Fingers

MY JUDE HAS PLACED THEIR PROMISE around my index finger.
It is a simple ring. Made in Seattle. Thin, silver, with tiny bands of gold.
Jude's promise is fresh; it is mine, a new memory in place of Ghost's.
Jude's ring will act as a barrier between my life and Ghost's. My Jude, a
tank with stormy eyes, can weaken Ghost's ties to my body. My Jude
ensures that I am able to breathe my own song.

My hands are thin, with long, wiry fingers that resemble dancers.
They are always moving, dipping up and down, uncertain of how to
rest. When I hear the skipping keys of a piano, these fingers, my fingers, flutter and prance, and Ghost burrows herself deep into the cave
of my belly, cooing with pleasure. She drapes her fingers over the lids
of my eyes so the piano ballad takes hold in the dark.

Beneath Jude's engagement ring, which holds dreams of cool water
and heated air, of beetles and fir trees, Ghost's tale of the piano song
she learned by ear curves around my finger bone.

In a darkened pub there is a deep-bellied piano with stained keys.
Across from the piano are pool tables with soft green tops and shiny

coloured balls. This is where the boy stands, face muddled in concentration while Ghost's fingers dance over the piano's teeth, slipping over thin black keys and fat cream ones. She pauses, guzzles her dizzy drink, and returns to the piano. Her fingers remember; they soak in the song, they soak in her breath. This is where Ghost plays her song, the one she knows by ear.

Nowadays my fingers are learning to prefer other things, like the gentle texture of a woollen blanket or a warm cup of coffee when the temperature outside is sinking. My fingers dance over my own memories—in the sweet, dark tunnel of Jude's sheets, or in the thin laces of my running shoes. My fingers are mine; they have their own song and their own gold ring.

$\mathcal{L}$

The second hospital looks just like the first. The tiles are the same, the RNS are the same, the gurneys, the colours, the patients—except this hospital has red numbers over the doors.

Ghost is a puppet now; her arms and legs flop, her head flops. Hands like small fish flipped over her knee, over the chair's plastic arms. They lie flat as the IV is inserted into her vein and pills are swallowed and more pills are swallowed and the light dims. Her body falls away.

The boy drums an invisible beat on his knee. After the light dims, he waits in the dark, wrapped in a blue blanket, and watches Ghost sleep, watches her breathe, listens to the heart monitor sing. Mama is there too.

Laid out flat, Ghost asks the boy to contact her school.

He takes her hand, he takes her phone.

"It's important. You have to do this now. Tell them I'm sick. I can't move my hands, you have to do this," Ghost whispers.

"What's your password?"

"Seven ... two, umm, five, umm, nine?"

The boy sighs, but he is holding her phone. The lights are low, the air is throbbing.

This story is in Ghost's finger bone, wrapped in tendons under the skin. When she sings of the hospital, of all the RNS and the blinding lights, she radiates.

The hospital is dressed like an old church, ancient and still, like the ones you see on television where the stained-glass windows allow in a few threads of light and the only sound is the visitors' breath. Ghost is in her gurney, legs tossed askew, arms folded across her chest.

Mama gently caresses Ghost's hand. The boy kisses her cheek. The RNS take notes and wheel her from one room to the next.

Now Mama and the boy are both sitting around the bed, Ghost's audience, hands folded sternly on their laps, speaking to one another in whispers.

"They're going to do another angiogram," the boy says.

"And surgery?"

"I don't know. I haven't even seen a doctor yet, they just keep sending her for tests."

Ghost is still, her body limp and her breath heavy. Each inhale, each exhale pervades the room, slipping into all the cracks and crevices. Ghost's mama leans forward, her neck outstretched toward the bed; she cups Ghost's hands, gently squeezes her fingers.

The boy leans back in his chair—he is always in a chair, in every hospital, in all of Ghost's stories, he is in the same position, waiting. In the background, silently waiting, watching her body, watching the wall, sitting for hours, waiting. And the church lights flicker, and the audience moves and buzzes around Ghost's bed, which now includes a bustling hive of RNS with clipboards and timelines and more tests and further results.

When the doctor arrives, the audience quiets down. Mama clears her throat, and the boy looks up from his phone.

"So, the test results came in, and I have reviewed them."

Ghost stirs. Her tiny body vibrates under the cream blanket, her fingers tap an invisible beat.

The doctor is young. He has a perfectly trimmed beard and soft skin. His voice flows over the chaos, over the audience, over the fluorescent lights. He kneels down so his eyes are level with Ghost's.

"You have what is called an arteriovenous malformation."

Ghost's fingers still, and her eyes are wide.

"It's an abnormal tangle of blood vessels in your brain. Something you were born with and that has erupted. The measurement for AVMs ranges from grade 1, the smallest, to grade 5, the largest. Yours is size 4."

"Oh. It is big," says Ghost.

The doctor agrees, and the audience murmurs.

"Because I am not trained in treating AVMs, I am unable to operate on them, but I have a friend on the mainland who works on AVMs at Vancouver General Hospital, and he can help you. He's a very good neurosurgeon. You'll be transferred there tonight."

And then the doctor is gone. Then Ghost is in the hallway, lying on a gurney.

An RN swings by to collect Ghost for her next exam.

"You'll have to remove your piercing." The RN points to her own upper lip to help Ghost understand what she means.

Ghost's hand flounders. Her fingers slide over her lip piercing.

Her mama and the boy have disappeared.

"I can't," Ghost mumbles. "I can't," she says again.

✣

The room is moving back and forth, back and forth. A sharp vibration that blends shapes until everything is softer, far away.

"Are you sexually active?" a man in blue asks Ghost, whose head is still wobbly.

"Yes."

"You'll have to take a pregnancy test before we begin."

"I'm not pregnant," she mumbles.

"Are you sexually active?"

Ghost pauses. "Yes."

"Then to be safe, you must take a pregnancy test."

Ghost is quiet. She doesn't tell the man in blue that her boyfriend is not cisgender, that he does not carry sperm, that the odds of her being pregnant are zero percent. So instead, she flops her head from one side to the other, accepts the plastic sample cup, and asks for the boy, who has been watching the scene for some time now.

"I'm here," he says and guides her to the nearest restroom.

Nuzzled against the restroom wall for balance, Ghost urinates all over her fingers, all over the floor, all over the plastic cup, until it is filled. The walls are throbbing, fading in and out to Ghost's song.

Two, three, four, five.

Her failing body pressed against the wall.

Two, three, four, five. "I am not pregnant," she tells the boy.

The boy helps to screw the cap on the cup. Helps to hold Ghost up. Helps Ghost out of the hospital restroom and back down the hall.

"I am not pregnant," she tells the boy again.

"I know," he says as he hands the plastic cup to the man in blue.

CHAPTER 25

Medicine

IT IS AFTER SUPPER WHEN JUDE TELLS ME they're considering taking hormones. The silver moon is half hidden by the murky clouds, and the winds are sweetly singing. Ghost is sweetly singing.

"It's microdosing," they say, carefully laying out the words.

And I nod, I nod.

"I want enough to lower my voice and square my jaw. I want people to be uncertain when they see me. I want people to not know what gender I am, but that's all. Then I'll stop."

And I continue nodding.

Their cologne, holding memories of the Italian beach, once again tickles my nose, calls me forward until we are lips against lips, heat breathing heat. I hold Jude, I hold all their words and all their thoughts and all of our worries.

"When will you begin?" I ask, my fingers tracing their hairline.

"I don't know. I still have to talk to the doctor."

The boy told me that he'd begun taking hormones when he was in his thirties. At the beginning, he'd worried that the process of transitioning was a ticket for the lucky ones who were young and spritely, but a missed opportunity for him. But that all changed after he spoke with other ticket holders, who assured him that age was not an issue.

✍

When Ghost whispers the story of the boy and his medicine, she reaches deep down and presses her fingers against my cranium. Her story, folded three times and blanketed in muscles, is kept safe, always protected. There is a distant road surrounded by long stalks of stark, golden grass held in place as the wind holds its breath. Across the way is a barn with faded walls, looking like a natural part of the grass field. There is a bus stop where Ghost and the boy wait, leaning against the metal pole, their arms damp, and then sitting on the curb, their legs stretched out over the sidewalk, because the bus is late and the dizzy drinks are wearing off.

The sun paints the streets in gold, and the smell of warm dirt is pervasive, on my lips, on my tongue. In this memory, I can taste Ghost.

"I think I want to start taking T," the boy says. The small golden vines hanging from the willow trees above the dried grass are frozen still. And then we are in the kitchen. The lights are dim, and the television fizzles in the background. Ghost is on her knees behind the boy as he faces the little silver coffee maker with his hands on the counter, his face relaxed. Ghost squeezes his right glute and slips the end of the hypodermic needle into his flesh.

Ghost and I are both aware that medicine is a silent act of bonding between people. A form of love. Ghost administers the boy his injections and, in turn, after that day in November, the boy gives me my pills.

He carefully slices the pills into quarters and halves, counting the pieces and organizing the dusty fragments into piles for each day. He adds yellow ones and medium-sized ones, he sets a timer and brings me tall glasses of water to swallow along with the tiny gifts. He watches me to ensure that all are taken and none are lost.

One of the pills is called dexamethasone. It is to be taken every four hours. The dexamethasone is first given to Ghost to keep the vessels in her brain from ballooning further. To freeze them in time. Every four hours, for weeks, she swallows a small white pill. After the surgery, the nurses fill a small bag with pills and give it to the boy. The doctors instruct him to feed me one every four hours at first. They also ask the boy to eventually wean me off the dexamethasone; it needs to be slowly phased out. So the boy is to cut each of these pills in half and then into quarters. He is to ensure that every few hours, I swallow my medicine.

Another set of pills is prescribed for every six hours. These are larger and not to be cut. These pills regulate my pain and make me sleepy. I can feel this medicine rummaging through my veins, filtering my thoughts into non-existence, into a place between life and death, a beautifully faded photograph of stillness. My body slips into the grey labyrinth of the murky unknown, resting against emptiness.

The dexamethasone drives a hunger in my belly, so the boy has to feed me constantly. He heats cans of soup and frozen television dinners for me. He makes me split pea soup, chicken noodle soup, vegetarian chili. My right hand, still weak, shakily shovels the food into my mouth. My lips grab the spoon for balance as most of the soup drips down my chin and onto my chest.

"I can't remember. Do I like this?" I spit.

The boy is hunched over, feverishly wiping the counter. He pauses briefly. "Does it taste good?"

"Yes."

"Then you like it," he says.

And my stomach growls as Ghost continues to sing.

❧

Jude and I talk beneath the covers, by the window where the green-budded trees are no longer skeletal. Jude's cologne is filling my lungs with the promise of life.

"I'll only be taking a small amount." Their thick arm reassures me. "The needle I have to use looks thick. I can give myself the shot in my belly or my thigh," they tell me excitedly.

I picture a needle the size of a turkey baster, thick, round, grotesque.

"Do you want me to give you your shot?"

"No, thank you. This is something I need to do myself."

Jude's words sting.

"I'm so proud of you," I tell them.

"You're not upset?"

"No. I'm just proud."

But Ghost is upset. I can feel her hands pushing my throat, because we both know that medicine becomes a tradition or a celebration, and this is what lovers do, this is what bonds them.

Ghost begins digging for memories of the boy, of her big pills. Her fingers burrow in the small areas of my body, beneath the thickened muscles. I hold my breath, grimace through the burning sensation that Ghost is causing. Burning, burning. I hold my breath and slip away.

❧

Each Sunday, after the sun has set, the boy receives his hormones. I watch from the living room, curled up on the black pleather sofa, body cocooned in the royal-purple throw blanket as the boy's friend, Becky, kneels on the hardwood floor and injects him with hormones. And Ghost squirms as we watch, her nails dragging down my ribcage, her chest erupting in pain. Becky has been doing the injections ever since

Ghost went into the hospital. Ghost is angry that someone has taken over her job.

"I want to try." Ghost's words slip out in a tone so loud and deep that it startles the boy and Becky.

"You can try next weekend," he says, his voice hopeful.

So the following Sunday, I join the boy in the kitchen. He fills the syringe with the special fluid and faces the little silver coffee pot. And Ghost stretches her fingers, and I stretch my hands, because it has been a long time, and we both hope that this body will remember.

My right hand, the one that feels like it's filled with exploding stars, grips the needle as I balance on my knees on the hardwood floor, just like Becky did. The boy grips the kitchen counter.

"Ready?" I ask.

"Yup, remember to squeeze tight and I won't feel the needle," he says.

I squeeze his glute with my left hand, the strong one.

"Yep, just like that," he says. Ghost grabs my hand because we both know this is her job.

My right hand—still numb, still unable to do things like the other hand—clutches the tiny needle in a fist. We ignore the stars. We move past the numbness as the needle plunges forward, breaking the boy's skin, meeting the resistance of his muscles—and then we pause. The needle shaft is a quarter of the way in and refuses to move further. It's stuck, wobbly, just below the surface of his skin. I have to push it in farther; the needle is supposed to go in all the way, just like how Becky did it. Just like Ghost used to do it. I breathe out and feel Ghost slither down, away from the boy, because they can no longer dance together, and this celebration, this tradition is no longer.

My left hand releases the grip on his glute to help finish the job, to push the needle in fully and inject. But the action is not smooth. I can't control the needle. It is too heavy, and my right hand isn't working. I grip the needle with my left hand and yank it out.

"Fuck," the boy says with a grimace, gripping the counter tight, small beads of sweat decorating his arms. "That hurt."

"I'm sorry," I tell him.

Ghost is kicking my insides, squeezing my heart and temples and vessels and bones.

"I'm sorry," I tell her, as the boy sighs.

I hand him the syringe, watch him pull up his pants, and follow him to the sofa in the living room.

"You pick something to watch on television, okay? I'm going out for a smoke." He grabs his pack and swings out the front door. I can hear his heavy tread on the wooden steps. I can hear the balcony door swing shut. Ghost is wailing again, her screams filling my head, clouding my ears.

✒

In autumn, Jude and I visit our beach again and sit in the sand, bundled in jackets and mittens, quietly imagining the heat and the scent of ice cream as the sunset paints the sky a rich red with smears of pink and gold.

"This is nice," Jude says, wrapping their thick arms around me.

"This is nice," I agree. "I have given T before, you know. My hands are strong enough now. My dexterity is back."

Jude leans in close. "No, thank you. This is something that I need to do."

They will gift the needle's medicine to themself as a form of self-love. And within a year, changes are noticeable. When we pass by other people, there are second glances and uncertainty.

"They're guessing," Jude says with pride. "They don't know what I am."

And I squeeze their hand. Hold it close.

CHAPTER 26

Ghost and the Hospital Room

IN GHOST'S STORY, the trees that surround the hospital are dressed in red. I am sitting on a sturdy branch, peeking through a cloudy window into her room and listening patiently for the test results. All around me, the leaves flutter. Inside the room, a woman dressed in a silk zebra-print blouse and thick black glasses leads a group of young doctors over to Ghost's bed. One of the doctors' face blossoms like a rosy apple with excited eyes. Wrapped in blue blankets, Ghost bares her teeth like a good girl as the doctors come close.

"Can you lift your arms, please?" the zebra lady asks.

And Ghost reaches both of her hands up to the sky.

"Very good. And can you touch your nose with your finger, like this?" Zebra lady demonstrates, lifting her arm and easily touching her fingertip to the end of her nose. The doctors lean forward, clutching their pencils and notepads.

Ghost, still smiling, lifts her left hand and taps her lip.

"Let's try again," the zebra lady coos.

And the doctors write on their pads of paper. Their eyes shine.

Ghost lifts her other arm and tries again. This time, she misses her face completely.

The doctors stare. Ghost smiles.

"I can't find my nose," she says sweetly to the zebra lady, who tilts her head and presses her bright-pink lips together. A small murmur erupts from the team of doctors as their heads bow and their pencils begin scratching.

"Do you remember me?" the doctor with the apple face asks. He is young, he is hungry. He bites the eraser at the end of his pencil.

"No," says Ghost.

And the doctors scribble more words onto their pads of paper.

✧

But the boy threads each loose string from this story and stitches the pieces together. In his tale, the hospital room was bright, because it was still early, and the window by my bed was clean, with a view of Twelfth Avenue. Down below, cars rushed by carrying people to other places, and there was a small green field across the way. The boy says that a team of medical students stopped by briefly, but they were only quietly observing. When, over the phone, the boy replays his own memory, with clear, logical transitions from one moment to the next, I can almost see the world differently, as though through a crystal pool.

The boy remembers the one young medical student, but his face was not rosy. He did not look like an apple. In fact, his face was a milky colour, and he was calm and clear. Yes, that makes more sense. And his instructor, the zebra lady, was not wearing a patterned blouse. She had glasses and dark hair, but she was not dressed in casual clothes. She must have been wearing a lab coat, like the others.

And I was still as a statue. Frozen in time as the low rumble of the hospital rushed in and as Ghost's whining, the tinnitus, filled my ears. And the young medical student, the one with the milky face, asked me a question. He said he was curious about my symptoms, trying to understand how I felt.

"My arm is numb," Ghost sputtered, and then her arm shone as a zillion tiny sparks misfired. Small shooting stars zapped the nerves in her arm. And the doctors scribbled words onto their notepads.

CHAPTER 27

The Cherry Blossom Clouds

ʕʕʕ AFTER THE LEAVES FALL AWAY and the large clouds drip for days, I am invited to visit the doctor for my yearly check-in. He says that, for the first while, yearly check-ins are a strong recommendation. There will be one appointment to discuss my upcoming angiogram, another to do the angiogram, then finally an appointment to discuss any findings. During the angiogram, a sedative is injected into my veins. The doctors then insert a catheter into a blood vessel in my thigh and drive it all the way up to my left thalamus, my cerebellum, and finally my brain stem, where a special dye is injected through the catheter. The dye makes its way to the malformation so that the doctors can see the AVM in an X-ray image of my brain. They can check to see if everything is still and make sure that I am safe.

The hospital is on the mainland, on a busy street surrounded by trees. The angiograms are nice. They insert a small IV into my right hand flush and send an opiate into my bloodstream. As I lie there in my drug haze, floating in the warm dusk, just a particle among looming, gentle clouds, the technician's voice snaps me back into the world.

"Turn your head right," he says, and I let my head fall to one side.

And then I float back into the clouds, the sweet cherry blossom clouds, into the special place where I was born. It is somewhere in between a memory and a faraway place. Not a painful place, just small and hidden. A place you can reach, but don't remember how to. This is where, deep within my brain stem, a small part of the AVM remains untouched, still active. But everyone agrees that because I am still young and the vessels are too flimsy, it's best to leave this bit alone. This is where I bled out slowly in November.

"Turn your head to the left"—and my head flops in the opposite direction.

So every year, I will come to have my blood tested and to float in the cherry blossom clouds. First, Ghost and I sit in the blue plastic chair and stare at the ceiling, at the tiny dark flecks on the tiles, at the technician in the white lab jacket peeling back the plastic casing from a needle and tightly binding my arm. The metal points is pushed into my arm, and my blood is drawn for testing.

Breathe, two, three, four ...

Vial upon vial is filled with dark liquid. Ghost even stops her wailing as the clear plastic tubes fill with our blood.

Breathe, two, three, four ...

On the day that Ghost died, after the form of treatment, embolization, was decided, Ghost was asked to sign some papers giving permission for the surgery to take place. The boy remembers the paperwork as long winded, written in small type, and difficult to understand. Ghost agrees. She says that the paperwork is blurry. But the boy and her mama tell her that this is for the best. So she signs her name on the important documents with a fountain pen that lives on the large desk in the waiting room of the hospital.

"What is this for?" Ghost asks again.

"For your surgery," says the boy.

"Oh. Okay."

She signs her name with uncertainty, while the boy chews his lip in concern, maybe questioning the decision internally.

And then Ghost asks her mama, "What is this for?"

The morning of the surgery, the RNs remind Ghost that she must rest. She cannot have water or food. The only medications to take are the large pills. She waits.

When the sun goes down, an RN helps her wipe herself down with Sage brand wipes to cleanse her body of bacteria. Ghost is brought on her gurney to the lower level of the hospital and given anaesthetic that seems to lift her up to the moon. Meanwhile, two doctors make a small incision on the interior of her upper thigh. The spot that the boy once kissed. Her special spot. A thin tube is inserted into her vein and driven up her groin to the "problem spot" in her left thalamus.

While they are directing the tube, the surgeons watch screens that show an X-ray of her brain. The images show the surgeons that the problem area is bigger than expected. In Ghost's brain, the pooling blood from her weakened vessels has created balloon-like structures called aneurysms, and when these burst, the blood gushed into her brain and caused damage. She has several aneurysms and a bleed from her cerebral cortex into her brain stem.

Ghost is not afraid; she does not mind at all. Right now, she is swimming beside the moon, swallowed by stars, her body hidden in the warm, dark breath of the night. The doctors send Ghost into the cherry blossom clouds while the thin, flexible tube drives into her brain and begins the slow and steady work of embolization. They use a special glue, Onyx, to caulk the broken areas, filling each of her paper-thin vessels so that blood can no longer run through them. It takes hours. The clock ticks, and the team of specialists focus. And Ghost swims high above it all.

CHAPTER 28

The Snow

THE SNOW SOFTENS EVERYTHING. Jude and I are holding hands, grasping one another, eyes darting down to our feet as we avoid the small patches of ice on the sidewalk. Light flurries dance across the pearlescent sky. My boots are tall, mid-calf, with the lusty sturdiness of serious horse-riding attire. They slush through the ash-coloured snow, keep my feet dry, grip the ground with their grooved bottoms, ensure my safety with each stride. We pass the hair salon—glossy posters of serious-looking women with high cheekbones, pouty lips—and the thrift store—windows lined with mannequins in sparkly vests and lime-green tube tops.

"We should stop in after," I suggest, squeezing Jude's hand and pointing at one of the mannequins.

"Tomorrow would be better. Let's go get a coffee, then afterward we can have dinner. Does that sound good to you?"

"Oh yes. Of course."

The mannequins' painted eyes follow me and Jude as we pass their store, their bodies bent in a frozen dance moves, like one of Ghost's photographs.

"I'll need to get some things from the grocery store. I know what I want to cook tonight. Spaghetti bolognese—doesn't that sound nice?" Jude smiles.

Jude always has an idea for what to cook. They are precise and know exactly what their body requires. Sometimes Jude tells me to choose a recipe; I believe they think it's good for my mental health. On these afternoons, I collect Jude's cookbooks from their small metal shelf. I flip through rich photos of freshly baked bread and chicken cordon bleu, of meals all laid out on tables, complete with velvet table-cloths and sprigs of pine. Picking a recipe is difficult. I much prefer having Jude decide.

"I can grind coffee while you cook," I offer.

"Why don't you relax? Take a bath."

"I want to help."

"You can clean up afterward, if you like."

Jude slows their pace as we tread up the hill on Spring Street. The thin streaks of cloud are already disappearing as we pass a beige-stone restaurant whose fluorescent red sign hints of sweet and spicy warmth.

"Let's eat here one day," Jude says to me as we pass.

I smile and squeeze their hand gently in response, because this is how Jude and I communicate.

Inside, the coffee shop is bustling with people—students with papers strewn across the tiny round tables and other lively folk spilling their stories to one another.

"Why don't you find somewhere for us to sit?" Jude says, peeling off their leather gloves, their scarf, their toque. Ghost's icy teeth are already biting my neck beneath my scarf, preventing the heat of the coffee shop from entering my bones.

I kiss Jude, struggling to ignore Ghost's painful nibbles as I remove my scarf. I want to fill my mouth with something soothing, to feel a warm, sugary rush. "Chocolate croissant?"

"Always chocolate," they say with a smile.

My eyes scan the room for a table. "And a coffee."

Jude's eyes follow mine across the room, surveying the tables of girls with shaved heads and hoop earrings, the lone woman sitting with a stack of papers and a reusable coffee mug.

"There's one." They point to the back of the shop, at a hidden corner behind a table of bright-eyed boys, their lips glossed and their shirts highlighting their chests.

"And oat milk." I swivel toward the empty table, passing the lone woman and the sultry-lipped boys, finding solace beneath the lights that gleam over the table, giving me a halo and dressing me in a brightness that makes me look like everyone else, like someone who is safe, who is normal.

A smooth-lipped boy in a blue sleeveless top screams across the table to his friend: "No, never, I had an internship!" And the table erupts in laughter.

Across the way, Jude is pushing past the tables, mugs in hand, skirting people whose chairs need to be pulled in.

"Your croissant is in the oven," Jude says, placing the mugs down. Their earthy perfume soothes me.

"I'm thinking we'll have pasta tonight," they repeat, because they understand this is something that may always have to be done.

"I remember."

And the beautiful ones sitting at the table beside us burst into laughter.

Jude cooks recipes from books and magazines. They tell me that cooking has been their outlet for years. While they cook, they listen to records and sing along. They pair various tastes from memory. Pasta sauce with a pinch of cinnamon, salted noodles, fresh basil, various greens and butter because that was the way they were taught by a lost boy somewhere in SF. They sharpen their knives and slice vegetables into perfectly round coins while the water boils and the oil simmers.

"Why don't you relax?" they offer again. "Dinner will be ready in about an hour."

Jude's yellow bathroom is small and smells of warm, musty cedar. Sometimes I close my eyes and imagine the forest. My body surrounded by warm pools of water that steam the mirror and promise safety. Outside the bathroom, Jude is singing and the clinking plates sound as though they are cheering as Jude stacks them. Each one placed carefully on top of another in a small pile by the sink. Sitting in the bath at Jude's house is one of my favourite spots, especially in the cooler months, when the icy wind begins to call.

&

After I'm sent home from the hospital, there's a game the boy and I play. I ask him questions about Ghost, and he answers.

"Do I enjoy cooking?"

"Yes."

"What type of food?"

"I don't know, all types. I guess vegetarian, though I'd much rather you made something else."

This body remembers some things. It remembers that vegetables must be washed and that I need a cutting board and that root vegetables must be sliced into smaller pieces so I can fit them into this mouth.

So one day, Ghost and I go by ourselves to the grocery store to buy vegetables. The boy is at work cleaning other people's homes, the type of people who gift cases of beer and home-baked biscuits around the holidays. There's a list of exercises I'm supposed to work on, but Ghost's sadness is wet and heavy, filling up my body and sloshing my tonsils and the roof of my mouth. The pills help; they offer a sleepy escape, but by midafternoon the medication wears off, and the hours begin to crawl across the floor again. When this happens, Ghost awakens in a sad and restless state. She pokes my ribcage with her bony toes while I watch the boy's cat, while I watch teenagers in wide-brimmed hats and loose pants playing hooky across the street, while I watch continuous episodes of a television show about a mother and her daughter who live in a quaint town with gentle problems.

The day Ghost and I go to the grocery store, we wait until the haze of medication lifts, until the sadness returns. I drag myself to Ghost's closet, behind her bedroom door. Her shirts and pants are strewn about, making the closet resemble a bird's nest of fabrics. The sun is pushing against the doors, the walls, sprawling across the floor.

Ghost's sweatpants are tight against my body, but I stretch them over my hips, my ass, and drop them to the ground. We pull on her jeans and fumble with the fastening. Our fingers flop against the gold button over the zipper again, again, again. And the trees peer through the large windows to see if I am capable, because they know that Ghost was. The thin buttonhole is too small, and these hands, my hands, are too large. Ghost grunts, her pool of sadness turned to anger. It gathers in my eyes and streams down my face, bleeds out of my armpits as finally, I manage to grab the flat button and push it through. The trees have lost patience, ruffling their leaves, and the sullen sun sinks lower.

Ghost is beaming now; she bubbles her sadness into the feeling of almost, the feeling of desire, the feeling of hope, and she bursts through each one of these vessels until she is dripping, dripping, dripping down into my cheeks.

I take a seat at Ghost's desk and study my face, focusing on the small pimples that decorate my cheeks and chin. The tiny black marks across my nose. The thick hairs above my lip. When I look into my honeyed eyes, the world shifts, and a feeling that lives deep down, somewhere in this body's brain stem, fizzles, because Ghost does not appreciate when I look into her eyes. She is not ready to see me yet. So, out of respect and fear, I look down at the desk instead, at the various tubes and containers of makeup.

Ghost takes my hand, almost as a peace offering, and reaches for a tube with a long golden lid. Her hand, my hand, grips the object and pulls it near. Her thin fingers float over my bones, aligning themselves with my touch to help me remove the lid.

Twist, two, three, four.

Our hands shake. The well-tightened lid doesn't give at first, then it does.

"This takes practice," Ghost tells me as I shut one eye and lean toward the mirror, careful not to look into her eyes. Black eyeliner. Ghost's eyes are always decorated with thick, bold lines, carefully smeared. But the makeup is in a different hand now. I grip the lid with its built-in brush, but it shakes and dabs, leaving dark clumps of liner on my eyelid and upper cheek.

Suck it up, buttercup, I think. Ghost throws the brush against the mirror with my right hand, which is still full of with explosive stars that spark and shock my system, small pricks against the soft padding of my palm. It is as if I have sat on it for too long and the blood is now rushing back, activating the nerves, sparking life. I wrap my left hand, the useful one, around the brush layered in black goop, and try again, leaning forward to see, but the dainty brush, made for girls like Ghost, shakes free from my hand, again dabbing my face and leaving clumps

under my browbone. Ghost is displeased, but now we both understand that these eyes will not be decorated today. Instead I empty her
drawers and toss shirts and sweatpants to the floor until I find her soft
grey toque. I rub my left-hand fingertips beneath my browbone, rub
the clumps of black until they are almost gone, faded.

And the clock ticks.

And the sun is beginning to fade.

And Ghost helps me grip a thin, slippery pencil to write a list.

Brcli

Potat

Orn

And the sun is wavering and Ghost is squeezing my temples and
dull pain blossoms.

I cram the piece of paper with the jagged pencilled words into my
pocket and put on my boots, which have zippers and Velcro. Ghost's
shoes are painful, complex, too tiny, so Mama purchased these boots for
me. They cup my feet and don't pinch my toes like Ghost's shoes do.

✌

Not long after I first arrived at the boy's apartment, he took me for a
walk. That day, the sun was shining, even though it was so cold you
could see your breath. My medicine made me warm, so even though
it was frosty, with strong gusts of sea air, I wore only a light hooded
sweatshirt. Other people were bundled in thick scarves and woollen
jackets, their hands wrapped in mittens, their heads in toques. The
air held only a hint of winter's sharpness; it bathed Ghost in freshness. That day, the boy tied the laces of Ghost's black-leather boots

and zipped up my sweatshirt. He wrapped his strong arms like tree branches around my waist and carried me down the stairs and held the door open and gently grasped my arm for my balance. But not long after we started walking, Ghost began biting my heels, digging her sharp claws into my skin, until I finally cried out.

"I can't walk, it hurts!"

"We have to walk home then," the boy said with a sigh.

"No. I'm okay. We'll walk slower," I grimaced and pushed Ghost and the sharp bits out of my mind.

✒

I stumble out the apartment door and, with both hands, grip the handrails of the steep staircase leading down to the front entrance of the building. My knees are still unsure of how to bend, how to help the rest of my body to balance. After each step, my feet pause, one waiting for the other to join it on the same step before trying the next one.

At the hospital, the RN had asked the boy about his home. "Do you have an elevator?"

"No, just stairs," he said.

"Will she have to use the stairs to exit and enter the building?"

"Yes."

"Are you home during the day to help her? Will she have to do it on her own?"

"I can help her," he said. "I only work until four o'clock, then I'm home."

When I finally reach the bottom, Ghost, with absolute pleasure, tickles my throat, kisses my cheek, and brushes my hair with her tiny fingers.

"You did so well," she whispers, and I smile and let her hot breath wash down my body, down our body.

Ghost and I walk to the grocery store. She knows the way; she pulls me down the street, past colonial homes and coffee shops. She is pleased today. The breeze is light and free. For the first time, my body feels strong, and I suppose that this is how it is supposed to feel.

It is dusk when I arrive at the store. It's crowded with other people rushing, rushing. They walk so quickly through the automatic doors, in front of me, behind me, past me. I am still breathless from the stroll, but Ghost is tugging at my arm, pulling me into the supermarket, toward the green baskets, the green carts, the lively people on invisible treadmills, rushing, rushing.

Near the entrance, the vegetables shimmer. Rich greens and yellows, crisp bodies proudly displayed in crates.

Rushing, rushing.

I want to crawl into the far shelf and hide among the padded loaves of bread. Ghost is singing with joy, squeezing my heart, licking my eyes. I slip my hands up over my ears and squint, listening to Ghost's whiny song as she leads me to the lush broccoli sprouts and then the rich-brown potatoes. She twirls me to the mushroom bin, digs my hand into the crate, and places handfuls of fungi into a brown paper bag. She pushes me toward the peppers, and we pause to fall into the hypnotic spell of the automatic sprayer before we stumble to the checkout line.

Rushing, rushing.

Breathe, two, three, four.

And beneath the darkened sky, Ghost and I make our way back to the boy's house. The plastic grocery bags are too heavy. They weigh my arms, pull my fingers, until cramping pain overrides the electrical sparks, over the joy of being strong, of playing. So I stop often to put down the grocery bags and stretch my hands, ball them into a fist and stretch them out again. Ghost is still proud because we are free again, and it's just me and her.

By the time I arrive at the boy's house, a long time has passed. The sun has set, and the grass is beginning to frost over. The boy is already back from work. He is sitting on the sofa, reading.

"I am going to make dinner," I announce.

He looks up from his book, his eyebrow raised.

"I will do it myself," I say sternly.

Ghost approves, her lips all over my heart, her fingers flicking my tongue, asking me to do this.

"Are you using a knife? I'll cut the vegetables." The boy marks his place in his novel.

"I'm going to do it all myself. I want to do it myself." My voice is raised and shaky and sounds younger than I want it to.

"Okay." He smirks.

But when I call the boy and tell him about this, he says that this is the wrong story. He says that he watched the sun set behind the mountains, and his heart was wretched with worry. That he called my cellphone, but I had left it in Ghost's bedroom, along with the door key, so he sat on the sofa and picked up a novel and counted the minutes on the clock above the television.

Just as he was making up his mind to begin searching the streets for me, I burst through the door, startling him. He says I was dishevelled and cross, my pants unbuttoned, my unwashed hair a wild mop.

I slammed the door shut and dropped my grocery bags onto the floor.

"I am cooking by myself!" I bellowed to the boy.

"I'll help," he offered and dog-eared his novel.

"No! I'll do this myself. Stay away from me! I don't want you in my way."

The boy says that the medicine I took made me very angry. He tells me that for the first time, he was afraid of me. So he sat back down and pretended to read his novel as he watched me prepare dinner. He watched me lift the blue plastic cutting board and slam it onto the counter. He watched me remove each vegetable from the grocery bag as if it were a misshapen stone and hard to grasp. He watched me wash the vegetables and lay their dripping bodies on the board. The knife was heavy and large. My palm pressed into the handle, and my fingers curled around it. I slammed the blade into a wet carrot, and a piece rolled across the board. I did it again. And again. And Ghost shook my eyes with glee until nothing was still, but I kept cutting until all of the vegetables were in jagged, misshapen pieces.

I asked the boy to turn the oven on, because I didn't understand numbers or what any of the buttons did. I just knew that it needed to be turned on. And he slowly rose from the sofa and came to press the buttons.

"It will beep when you can put them in," he said slowly. "I'll set the timer so you'll know when they're cooked."

✿

That night, the boy and I eat together at the kitchen table.

"I made this myself," I tell the boy, my cheeks glowing, my right hand shakily shoving vegetable coins into my mouth.

"You did, I saw," he says, taking small bites and using a knife to slice the bigger pieces.

"It was hard to cut," I say.

The boy laughs carefully. "I saw."

"Thank you for letting me cook. It was important."

The boy nods and takes another bite.

CHAPTER 29

The Mary Celeste

THERE IS A MYSTERIOUS TALE of a sailing ship that was discovered abandoned and floating aimlessly in the Atlantic Ocean during the nineteenth century. Her name was *Mary Celeste*. She had set sail from New York City in November 1872 and was scheduled to arrive in Italy in the following weeks, but she never made it. A month after she left port, she was discovered bobbing in murky waters, completely vacant. The ship's crew had vanished, yet all their belongings were still in their quarters, along with dishes of half-eaten food and clothes not yet worn. A postcard locked in time.

&

The day I board Ghost's vessel, the sky is smooth and empty. The trees hold their breath, the roads are closed in mourning. The boy and I stand in the doorway of her bedroom, studying her remains, her memories—everything is paused, as if she has only left for a moment.

Her seafoam-green duvet licks the footboard, crashing waves against metal. I gingerly touch her sheets, flop my hand over her soft pillow. Maybe once I lie down, smell her, touch my cheek to her pillow, Ghost will slither back into my bones and plump my skin with knowledge. I like her bed; it's so much nicer than the beds at the hospital.

Ghost's bedroom sets off a hymn found in the deepest part of my throat. It is mine now. There are tall, dusty windows that span the floor to the eggshell-white ceiling. All along the thick windowsills are paperback novels with worn spines. The books themselves hold their own secrets. Ghost is a collector; her room is filled with other people's stories, stacks upon stacks of other people's words. And as the sun filters into her room, I continue rubbing my palm over her bedsheets, allowing the soft cotton to swim under these fingers, to invite me home.

The boy is studying me. He knows for certain that something is different now.

Ghost is singing, her heart exploding, tugging my insides, looking for memories, pushing me toward her spot, past her large wooden desk scattered with makeup and brushes, with white stains and bits of powder rubbed into the ancient wood. A large mirror leans against the wall, the bottom balancing on the desk, surrounded by brightly coloured plastic bottles and vials. Tubes of lipstick, cakes of eyeshadow, and thick makeup brushes sprawl over the desk. Her desk. She pushes me past the windowsills that hold her books and into the corner, where her silver keyboard rests. The right side of my mouth tingles. Small electrical sparks, tiny bursting stars are burning up and down the side of my body as I look through the window at some teenagers on the benches below. How easily they swing their bodies, how carelessly they balance, as if it's nothing. And because of this, I despise them. It hurts, the envy I have for Ghost and her busy heart. I hate how easy she had it. How careless she was. How I lack everything that was natural for her.

"Home," I slur to the boy, who is still studying me with his oceanic eyes.

"You must be tired," he says cautiously. "I'll get your medicine, then you can get some rest, yeah? It'll be nice to sleep in your own bed."

The boy helps me remove Ghost's jacket, her pants, which strain against my stomach, and her shirt, which balloons over my breasts. He kisses my neck, leaving his smell, and carries my body to Ghost's bed, where I drift off to sleep for many hours and many days. I sleep while the sun disappears and reappears. Sleep paints me with molasses until I can no longer move.

⚬

But the boy has a different story about this day. He tells me that I did not fall into the night peacefully. Instead, I was belligerent and cold. His suggestion for rest hit my many nerves.

"You must be tired," he said cautiously. "I'll get your medicine, then you can get some rest, yeah? It'll be nice to sleep in your own bed."

"I'm not tired." My large tongue lolled around my mouth, unable to feel at home. "I want shower. I want shower on my own."

"Not yet." The boy's words were soft. "You have to wait until tomorrow, when I can help you."

"Why can't I on my own?"

"So that you don't fall. The doctors said that for the next little while, we're to do things together. To keep you safe. Lie down, and I'll get your medicine."

"I want shower," I repeated, but the boy had already left Ghost's bedroom and was now in the kitchen, in the hallway, rummaging through the pantry drawers.

And now I remember. He is right. I refused to sleep, and while the boy was in the kitchen preparing my medicine, I was seething, my mouth unable to hold its saliva, the right side of my face tingling.

Ghost began her wailing song. She sang the same screeching tune over and over again, about the loss of her boyfriend, the loss of her bedroom, her books, her makeup. She bemoaned her sudden death and promised, in her song, to never let me go, because if she was trapped, then so was I. Her high-pitched chords burned my ears even worse than the exploding stars that danced over half of my body. In the kitchen, the boy rummaged through the silverware to find a knife to cut the pills, cracked a beer to help calm his nerves, relieve the stress.

The boy says that, like Ghost, I am incredibly stubborn.

When the boy made his way back to Ghost's bedroom to give me my medicine and help me out of my clothes, he found me hunched over, hands grasping the wall to hold myself up. My back to the door, shaking and gasping, swallowing air. The boy carefully put down his beer on the dresser and made his way toward me.

"You're okay now. Why are you sad? I mean, before was scary, but it's all over now."

"It's hard. I don't ... it's hard."

He unbuttoned the dish-sized buttons on Ghost's blueberry peacoat.

"Raise your hands," he said.

And I raised them high to feel the air's warm breath as he slipped my shirt over my head, catching my ears, catching my nose. He swiftly popped the golden button through the buttonhole of my jeans and knelt down on the floor to slip them off me. Ghost, infuriated, was kicking my temples, squeezing my heart, digging her wretched nails into all of my muscles, until I had to squint. I felt my eyes watering again, felt them dripping.

"You're okay now, yeah?" The boy took a sip of beer. "You made it."

I stumbled onto Ghost's bed, pulled the blankets up to cover every inch of me. I didn't know this boy and couldn't tell if I liked him yet, but I showed him my teeth.

"Thank you," I drawled.

The boy handed me a whole white pill, watched me put it in my mouth, then passed me a glass of water and watched me swallow.

"We do full pills today and tomorrow, then half pills, okay?"

I watched the walls. I did not sink into the safety of familiarity. I watched the windowsills. I listened to Ghost's tune. I did this for days, for weeks, for months, because the night was empty, a timeless stretch of nothingness.

After the boy left Ghost's bedroom, he sat down on the sofa in the living room and watched television. He laughed, he ran the kitchen sink, he stepped outside for cigarettes. And I watched the windows. I watched the dust gather, and I listened to Ghost's song, which swallowed the heart that at the moment felt too large for my body. And when the boy returned, I met his eyes and slurred my words into a small, carefully crafted message.

"I'm sad."

"It's all over now. You should be happy. You made it."

And I continued to watch the dust gather and to listen to my Ghost sing.

CHAPTER 30

Jude's Feet

DURING THE WINTER MONTHS, when the temperatures dip and the air sharpens, Jude's feet and knees ache. When it is icy, their muscles clench, and the thick knots in the soles of their feet harden and press into the insoles of their boots. Jude says their broken limbs, their pain, are a badge of life experience, then they gently pull on my hand as their lips purse. This means we are to slow our pace. This means that they are feeling pain. Jude tells me that the soles of their feet were damaged in their twenties, somewhere in the Mission District, when they worked in the kitchen of a family restaurant.

"It was tiny. A small five-table joint. I would spend hours on the sanded tile, my feet constantly moving, soles burning," Jude says, their pace almost at a crawl.

This was after the Navy and before the 2008 recession. I remember this.

"My feet were burning, day after day." Jude shakes their head, eyes clouding. "It was me and three other guys all crammed in the back kitchen, no AC or fan, so we had to leave the back door open. We shared jobs. We all cooked and washed up in the same space. There were no mats to stand on, so my feet were on concrete for hours."

We are slowly creeping up Eighth toward our coffee shop, our place. Jude's gloved hand is wrapped around mine, our fingers linking, squeezing, to remind me that walking is an art form and must be taken in comfortable stride.

"This was in my twenties, so I'd numb the pain with beer. The guys and I would shut down the restaurant and drink their beer for a few hours after every shift. I didn't feel bad. The owners were these rich white jerks who didn't care about their employees." Jude tugs my hand back. And I sigh, because crawling up the street at this pace feels like my body, my Ghost, is in a cage. I am still able to shuffle quickly over the hard pavement without becoming exhausted, feeling fresh, feeling immortal.

When Jude winces in pain and slows us down even more, Ghost seizes the damp fabric of my lungs and pushes. She squeezes my heart, makes it skip, until my body is calling for the wind. I open my mouth wider to let more air in.

Jude slows their pace yet again as we tread up Spring Street. To the right is a hair salon, and beside it is the beige-stone restaurant with the fluorescent red sign.

"Are you hungry?"

My lips stretch over my teeth as I squeeze their hand gently. "Yes."

"I've been meaning to try this place with you," they say, backing into the front door to hold it open.

My lips meet Jude's cheek as I walk past them into the warmth of the restaurant.

my feet

🌿 IT WAS WINTER when the boy brought me in his orange-scented truck back to his home. The doctors recommended that he take me on short walks in the early evenings, when the sidewalks were clear. They suggested ten-minute walks. They said I would need to be patient and slow and allow the boy to guide me. And the boy responded with his fast-motored tongue while I stared at something invisible beyond the back wall.

For the first walk, the boy bundles me in the heavy blue peacoat and the thick grey toque. He ties a long woollen scarf around my neck and covers my mouth with it to protect my drooling lips from the frost. He takes my hand and leads me down the front steps. He wraps his hands around my waist, walking backward, his arms stretching out toward me just in case I tumble, just in case my feet also give up.

The night pools, and we stumble through her silent land. Even Ghost pauses her wailing to marvel at her beauty. Dew glistens on the neighborhood's lawns, hangs in the air, fills my lungs with life. And my

Ghost lurches me forward, playing with my body like a marionette—legs dancing to the right, to the left, jogging, tripping.

"Slow down!" the boy is calling, but my legs will not stop. These muscles must stretch and burn. These lungs must swallow the dewy droplets of life and gasp. Ghost understands. This is my acceptance, under the charred sky, swimming in the night. Past the thick houses and neatly trimmed lawns, past the cottage-style storefronts and mailboxes, around the corner, into the middle of the lane, gasping, gasping, beneath the street lamp.

"Slow down, please!" The boy's voice is tiny.

In the mornings, after the boy leaves for work, Ghost kicks my temples until my head swells and pulses. Three pills to calm my Ghost. Three pills every two hours to calm her nerves, make her legs heavy, numb the tearing sensation in my skull. Though the pills are not magic; the pain is still present, but it is manageable. These white pills calm Ghost until the early afternoon, and then I am to take three more, and then three more.

The boy's bathroom is tiny and spotless. There is a correct place for everything. He reminds me that the towels fit on the third shelf of the thin cupboard by the door. This is important to him and to the house.

"I'm sad," I tell the boy.

He nods.

I forget.

"The soap goes here," says the boy, and he points to the metal ledge above the bathroom sink.

"I am sad," I say, and Ghost continues her ballad, until the boy disappears.

In the mornings, after the boy leaves for work, after I introduce myself to his home again, I shuffle to his spotless bathroom. I turn the sparkly silver taps of the bathtub and test the water's temperature with my left hand. It is important that I use my left hand, because my right is still filled with exploding stars and cannot be trusted with these important tasks. The side of my body is made of stars cannot feel the temperature of the water, so only the left half, the part that is part of this world, can warn me if it's too hot, too cold, can melt beneath the warm water.

My face no longer droops and when I smile. Because of this, the boy is comfortable letting me do things on my own again. He says I look like myself again, except for my eyes. In photographs, Ghost's eyes are like a honey-coloured vase holding something secret, something untouchable, but my eyes—they are gentle, they are safe. The boy is aware that something is different. He knows that something is out of place. He tells me that Ghost visits him after he has fallen asleep. She tells him that she is still here. When the boy says this I look away because we both know that I am unrecognizable. An imposter.

But I dream of Ghost too. Sometimes she drags me under her tongue, allows me to watch her wandering through an old beach resort with solemn umbrellas wavering, their fabric torn. She walks slowly, not looking for anything in particular, just pacing down each empty avenue.

After the boy leaves for work, after I take my bath and swallow the white pills that make my Ghost dozy, I walk. Small walks at first. Short trips up and down the street. Floating down the old staircase of the apartment building and past the muddy lawns that surround the colourful homes of Gladstone Street. Up and down the street, uncertain of direction or where I am. My right foot is full of stars, unable to fully move in this world, and my dizzy eyes, licked by Ghost's medicated tongue, hang heavy, forget how to see, so the coloured houses vibrate, and the ground is never steady. But I must walk to the muddy grass and then back to my home and up the great staircase.

And then, and then, again.

Each day I walk a little farther, until I finally reach the small park across from the row of homes with brick chimneys, clean windows, and blue shutters. My body sore, my lungs gasping, I sit on the lone bench and look out at these homes, which seem to be empty. Ghost is happily strumming my heart, because she enjoys walking and smelling the sea air. She wants to feel free, to taste life.

And so Ghost and I walk for most of the day. Past coffee shops and the mint-green house with the cedar-coloured chimney, under the mountains and the faded sky, down the dirt path bordered by shrubs that winds beside the ocean, where Ghost's salty lips dance over my neck, her excitement playing in my throat.

In the early evenings, before the boy gets home, I walk to the community garden on the edge of the street. I sink onto the warm wood of the garden bench, sucking in the floral scent, pressing my fingers into a hanging leaf, rubbing it between my fingertips until it stains my nail green. I want the garden's memory inside of me, to keep Ghost happy, to keep her calm.

The doctors have recommended that I take everything slowly, that I not consume too much at once. So I ask the garden to calm my heart, control my breath, and I watch the plants slowly sprouting. Witness the long green flower stems bending in the wind. I sit for hours, letting the sun heat my skin, letting the rain soak me. I focus on the leafy plants on the other side of the garden and the tiny, busy insects.

Ghost is happy here. She reaches up, her hands clogging my throat, and attempts to grab onto the sky and find her way back. Her warmth radiates through my hand as the buzzing of the stars pulsates through my body and shatters my frame. The rich, dark aroma of coffee tickles my senses, layered with the crisp sound of dried leaves cracking beneath my shoes after a frost, and the way, in the summer, the stained-glass window in our bathroom shines like a handful of jewels.

In the garden by the boy's house, Ghost slips her fingers deep down into the pit of my stomach and unearths Mama's garden, which has tough old dandelions and wild sunflowers that reach toward the sky. She goes deeper, until her fist is grinding and my own hands are gripping the edge of the garden bench, my eyes softening until all the petals fade into one another and streak across the sky.

Mama's garden bed is thick with various weeds. Ghost and I are lying down, staining our skin in the mud as we watch fleshy worms pop up their heads, their tails, then bury themselves in the rich soil, seemingly unaware of us, a giant sprouting clovers in our hair. At the edge of the garden near the fence are two large oak trees, their trunks rough and rippled. I stretch out Ghost's body beneath the tallest oak and dig my fingers into the soil, press my ear to the ground, and listen for the chatter of insects. Little Ghost is squealing with delight as the insects jig over her palms.

The sunflowers are warriors guarding the entrance to the garden, rigid and covered in sharp hairs. The grass is sharp, dehydrated; its itchy stalks poke and prod. We dance over the grass all the way to the white fence that Ghost and John painted. He'd rolled up the cuffs of her jeans. Both wearing canvas sneakers and large round glasses that glinted in the afternoon sun. Ripe brown beetles inhabit the floor of the garden. Ghost and I pluck fat **fruits** from a raspberry bush and suck the sweet juices, rolling the **seeds** over our tongues. I poke my palms against the yellow grass, now watching Ghost and John swiping their paintbrushes over the fence, watching the paint clump. As the sun sets, my skin, damp from the afternoon heat, cools itself. In the distance, a car door slams, and then there's laughter, and then silence.

CHAPTER 32

The Sun

GHOST'S MEMORY BOX holds a few photographs of John. In this one, I can tell it is a long time ago, because the colours are subdued, yellowed, and she is still a baby. With a wide grin, his eyes bulging with glee, John balances Ghost on his shoulders.

This was years before dance class, years before all of Ghost's stories. John has a story that has been slipped inside my skull, somewhere close to the area I am from. It is a loose, floating photograph: John, with a short, curly mop of hair, wearing faded jeans rolled at the cuffs and large gold glasses. Large front teeth. Red cheeks. He walks to and fro with the metal lawn mower, a confetti of grass falling around him. When Ghost whispers about this photo, she says she is ill. This is when John and Mama grow concerned and take her to the doctor, who runs a few tests but says that Ghost is growing, that these migraines are an unfortunate but sometimes common occurrence in young women.

In the backyard, near Mama's garden patch, Ghost lies on her back, the fresh air comforting her. A stack of pillows beneath her head to help ease the pain. When she centres her head just right she can sleep for a few hours in the sun, in the warmth, which is important, because the dark and the cold feel lonely. When her belly is empty, the sides of her tongue are weighted in bile, her lips painted with the residue of yesterday's dinner. She watches the clouds, and then she watches her bedroom ceiling. She stays still because she has learned that any movement will bring back the pain. Shallow breaths ensure that she does not move her body too much so that she can have a few luxurious moments of calm, of sleep, before the tearing sensation begins again. John visits; he takes her hand and pinches the area between her thumb and index finger, and Ghost says it helps. She no longer feels pain when he does this, and she falls asleep, lulled by John's magic touch.

Mama tells me that one day, a long time ago, John left the house with the garden. He left for a condo somewhere in the city, somewhere far away. She still has framed photographs of their wedding day—her nose dipping into a bouquet of roses, her eyes closed, dreaming of something nice.

"He was a good dad," she assures me.

And Ghost agrees.

"Where is he now?"

"I haven't talked to him." And then she is silent.

"He helped with the headaches, right?"

"Oh yes. And he took you to dance class. He was a good dad." She nods.

A similar tearing sensation gripped me after the boy and I left the hospital. It was winter, and the road was long and icy, but I remember the sun; it was warm that day. The pavement was golden, and there were long stalks of dried grass bordering it. The world was soft and empty except for me and the boy. We walked in silence for ages. This is how I remember the way home from the hospital. I don't remember the bus ride or the boat ride. I wore Ghost's running shoes. I wore her blue jacket and mittens. And the sun was shining, embracing me and welcoming me home.

CHAPTER 33

Haunted

🌿 I HAVE STARTED READING SELF-HELP BOOKS written by women with long hair and flushed cheeks who recommend that I find my inner voice, that I return home to myself. They say that authenticity is vital for happiness, the key to experiencing serenity laced with wisdom, but they don't have my Ghost. When these women speak of home, it's someplace soft, angelic. They write letters to themselves asking for peace, mailing forgiveness in gold-frosted envelopes on bone-white paper. I try to do these meditations, to ask my Ghost for forgiveness, but instead of playing a gentle tune and sitting quietly, she kicks my stomach, digs her nails into my neck, and refuses to find peace. She is already too big for the both of us in this body, and I am beginning to feel suffocated. My throat is unable to contain her, so I am spilling her secrets, her stories in lieu of my own.

My sweet Jude tells me that they do not enjoy Ghost's stories. We are at our coffee shop, spilling truths, peeling back ugly secrets. I suck in my bottom lip, release it, and take a deep breath, tapping my fingers against the wooden table, running them down its smooth indentations. Ghost is playing statue, freezing my muscles, tightening my jawline.

"We aren't meant to grip onto the past, it's unhealthy." As Jude speaks, Ghost stirs within my throat, so I grab my mug and take a giant sip of lukewarm coffee in hopes of quieting whatever she wants to tell Jude. I know it will be mean. I understand this now.

"It isn't fair," Jude continues, leaning forward to cover my hands with their own like a turtle shell. "You're obsessed and holding an expectation that I should be fine. I'm not. Do you hear me? I'm not okay with your obsession."

Outside, bright-eyed teenagers in loose-fitting jackets howl with laughter. Jude looks at me. I know I have to be honest, because this is what married people do: they share all of their secrets, each thread of vulnerability.

"I don't know if I can." My voice shakes, and I look away, toward the front entrance, past a woman in a floral dress.

"I can't share you," Jude says firmly. "It isn't right. You have a choice. I'm not going to give you an ultimatum, but I can't continue this relationship if you don't let go of him."

Ghost is wailing again. Breath out, two, three, four.

Jude does not like Ghost's stories about the boy. They say the stories are desires, that they are missed opportunities of the heart.

"He helps me see the way things used to be. We don't speak that often."

Jude takes a sip of coffee, wraps their large hands around the mug. Ghost is plucking my heart again, making it skip beats, because she does not appreciate Jude's opinions. To her, they are a swarm of locusts, a messy deal, a blur of discombobulated images that trap her even more.

Ghost tells me that the boy is the only one who understands what happened in the small grey room. That he witnessed the dimming of the lights. That he heard the noise and swam in exhaustion along with her.

And she says that I owe her.

I take a sip of coffee, let the sweet liquid wash down my throat, and try to find warmth in Jude's eyes, but their face is solemn.

"I can't say yes," I breathe.

And Ghost agrees, as the sun dances over the table and catches on the silver spoons at the edges of our empty plates.

"Jude?"

Ghost's hands press down on my tibias, holding my legs, telling me to look, look, look.

"It's your choice." Jude pushes their empty coffee cup forward. The teenagers have disappeared, leaving behind a lonely sidewalk and a closed-on-Sundays record shop.

"I still don't understand what happened," I tell them, and nothing else, because to say that I stole Ghost's body, which is filled with her memories, her stories, would sound bad. To tell Jude that sometimes the one I call Ghost makes me relive her tales until I am unsure what is real and what is false would make me certifiable.

Jude's smoky eyes stained with bits of plum glisten now, caught by the sun.

*

Jude's apartment is heavy with summer, whose tongue has licked the windows, leaving a filmy residue and a warm scent. The screaming man is somewhere else tonight; wandering with his worries down another city street, past different stores, different towers. Outside, the sky is dark, and I am in here, away from the stars that no longer reside in my arm or on my lips. Jude is drying cutlery, gently putting the dishes to bed.

"I used to paint," I call to them, attempting to break the silence, to drag us away from Ghost's issues.

"I know," they mumble, wiping their hands on a kitchen towel.

"In Philly, I was an artist."

Jude's hands are busy with the record player, then with their slippers, then with the crumbs on the dining table.

"There were goddesses in the water fountain, and fish spitting streams of water. They were stained with age. I would draw them."

I invite Jude to taste my Ghost.

"You've told me," they say, and that is all.

Ghost nods solemnly, her chin aligned with my own, and we return to the silence. The walls fade in and out as Ghost's sharp nails begin scratching. She drags her fingers across my neck, back and forth, back and forth, until I whelp and my eyes water.

I cover my eyes and breathe, two, three, four, five.

Ghost's wails reign louder still. Her thick elbows rail into my skull, beat against my temples.

I once saw a documentary on Netflix in which a soft-faced woman with high cheekbones and silver hair recommended breathing until your body was part of the act.

Two, three, four, five ...

She said that breath moved emotions like clouds.

Two, three, four, five ... She said that all at once, your body would transcend.

Two, three, four, five ... But she was in her own body, and she wasn't fighting with Ghost.

Two, three, four ... My head is pounding. Ghost's fists are hammering my skull.

"We'll figure this out," Jude promises.

I drag myself from the living room to the kitchen, listening to the soft pitter-patter of my socked feet against the tile.

"Will we?" I pour myself a glass of water and drink it.

I drink another glass.

I drink until I drown out Ghost and her screams.

I drink until my belly blossoms. A thick, round planet filled with water. I drink until Ghost suffocates. I drink until she is finally still, and then I waddle to Jude and fall onto their sweet lips, a familiar ache radiating from my head, from my midsection. Wiping the tears from my cheeks as I stagger into the warmth of their arms. The soft leather of their palms reaches down, rub the roundness of my belly. Their face entangles in my wild mane. With Jude, my body feels quiet and sweet.

Jude's breath hovers across my neck, trickles down my stomach.

"We will figure this out," I whisper back, my lips beneath theirs, mouth swallowing the promises of tomorrow, of tasting Italy and the dreams of our ancestors, of sealing a distant future that is our own, only our own.

CHAPTER 34

The Ring

ON THE EVENING OF GHOST'S DEATH, the maple trees rustle their reddened leaves and hold their breath. Inside the grey hospital, all the way to the eighth floor, the boy sits in a padded chair, stretching the hours—two, three, four, five—by stretching his legs, standing and pacing from one end of the room to the other, from one end of the hall to the other. And when that is finished, he returns to his seat and does it all over again.

On the sixth hour, he crosses his foot over his knee and looks up at the ceiling, focuses on the off-white tiles, and begins to count the small holes, just like Ghost once did.

On the seventh hour, the boy lifts his worn body and stalks up to the long desk in the middle of the hallway.

"You said three hours, yeah? She's been gone for much longer," he says to the RN managing the desk.

The RN looks up from her work. "When she arrives, I'll have someone come for you. Until then, please wait in the waiting area."

The boy looks at the clock for reference. "Are you sure she isn't back yet? It's been much longer than the doctors said it would be."

"When she arrives, I'll have someone come for you," the RN repeats.

"She was only supposed to be gone for three hours."

"When she arrives—"

The boy pounds his fist on the counter. "It's been seven hours. I just need to know that she's all right."

The RN looks at the boy, exhausted. "When she arrives, I'll have someone come for you." Her chin wobbles down, and she returns to labelling, to the computer, to her long list of patient notes.

"Fuck," the boy mumbles. "It's not all right."

Mama tells me by then, it was early evening. She was waiting as well, sitting with the boy in the waiting room in silence. After the seventh hour, she calmly watched him pull himself out of his chair and stagger to the front desk. She tells me that everyone was so exhausted, that exhaustion was the reason he pounded his fist on the front desk and raised his voice. She watched him fill to the brim, and then she swooped in and took his arm. She says he was frightened and tells me with pride that she smoothed over the tension. That when she was done, the RN understood why he was upset and the boy's eyes were less heated.

"I used to work in a doctor's office." She beams when she tells me the story. "I returned to work right after you were born. I know how it works. I know how busy it is. I know how it feels to work in a hospital."

In the waiting area, the boy looks up at the clock with large numbers on its face, looks down at the floor tiles, leans his head back, and closes his eyes to remove himself from the hospital. He imagines the waiting area drifting away. He floats up toward the clouds where Ghost is resting and runs his lips across her thighs until her warmth and skin are all he can taste. Because in the boy's dreams, Ghost is still warm, she is still alive. He holds her there, still, until every last bit of air leaves his body, until his heart is still as well. Around his neck on a chain is Ghost's mood ring. She told him that this ring had travelled through many states before finding itself against the boy's chest. And the boy promised to wear it, always. So he slips his fingers around the ring and rubs its smooth metal curves until his skin is raw.

He pictures Ghost in the operating room, flat on her back, full of tubes and a catheter, and for the first time in many years, he prays.

"Just let her live," he whispers.

From somewhere beyond the blossoming clouds, behind the moon, ears are piqued.

"I don't want to live my life without her, I can't bear it." The boy breathes in and out slowly. "But I'd give her up if you just saved her, I would," he promises.

And the ones who listening begin placing their bets. The boy breaks, his throat opening wide as he clutches the ring with his swollen fingers, because the love that he and Ghost share is a precious stone, highly sought after.

Halfway through the eighth hour, when the boy's lips are heavy, greased with his promises to the gods, the elevator door opens, and Ghost's gurney appears.

"Thank you," the boy whispers.

"Thank you," the gods respond.

And a scent that will turn the heads of many wafts down the hallway to greet the boy. The RN looks up from her thick stack of papers. "She's arrived."

CHAPTER 35

Ghost's Death

GHOST'S MAMA AND THE BOY ARE WALKING beside the gurney, stroking my arms, cupping my hands, leaving gentle notes in my ears as I swoosh from the end of the hallway to the other, into a dark, quiet room across from the nurse's station in the middle of the hallway.

My head is heavy, carrying the body of Ghost, still unsure of how to move or where she is. My legs and arms are disconnected pieces, a patchwork doll waiting for a spark to grant her life, to bring her into the real world.

"It's time for her to sleep," the RN tells Mama and the boy. "You can visit tomorrow."

The room is filled with sounds of the deep ocean, far beyond the shells, the sands, the muddy soil. The boy tells me afterward that when the RN asked them to leave, he raised his voice, he raised his displeasure, and then Mama laughs and tells me that, again, she calmed the situation, because rules are rules, and she understood that they must be maintained.

"I used to work in a medical clinic, I understand how hectic things can be."

The boy is tired. The RN is tired. So Mama and the boy kiss me goodnight and promise to come back after the sun rises. They leave sweet, gentle words of encouragement on the windowsill.

It is well past visiting hours, and after the boy and Mama leave, the hospital is silent as a sacred tomb. My body is held flat against the hospital bed by invisible hands, held in place by the night. The hallway lights dim, and a gentle roar erupts inside my ears. Here, I am between life and some other distant place, almost asleep, perched on the edge of this world, hypnotized by the music of the heart monitor. Cocooned in blue blankets, I toy with sleep, opening my eyes and closing them again and again, until I do not know which is which. I do not know if I am breathing. I do not know this body, this space, but I can feel her bony fingers wrapped around my legs, feel her mouth beside my ear, sucking in the tender farewells, consuming the words of her mama and the boy.

Ghost is on the edge of the gurney, her thin shoulders slumped forward, her back pointed, eyes narrowed. She traces my hairline with her fingers, kisses my cheek, and slips back into her bones to begin her busy work of burying each memory. She weaves stories of the church and the movie-star woman in the ribs, of kissed lips in the left clavicle, of the suburban sun, Philadelphia, her heart, her music, her dancer's feet. She buries the boy in her chest, she buries the boy in each part of this body. She is welcome to do this, to leave small untouchable threads of herself wrapped in this body, in my body, because the gods who granted the boy his wish, they enjoy the tragedy, they enjoy the entertainment.

When the skies lighten and dawn kisses the landscape, the tomb becomes a hospital. Ghost buries her last story somewhere in my throat; I am to think of her every time I speak. Her fingers dig into my calves until they are wrapped around my bones, then she sinks into my body.

Beyond the red-leafed trees, the sun swells. The boy and Mama awaken in their own homes. Mama surrounded by paintings of European streets markets, the boy at a hotel near the hospital. They each pack their bags and brew their coffee, the boy has a cigarette, and Mama toasts some bread. They each slip on their shoes and leave for the hospital. And Ghost begins her long-winded song laced with sorrow. She sings until the world fades away and I am smothered by her, trapped in a jar, unable to move or see clearly. She shifts the stage until there is only captivating night that smothers my airways, and she drags me into her dreams, because it's not fair and why should she stay all by herself when this was never her choice.

The day after Ghost dies, I watch the floor tiles sway, I watch from the bed as phone calls come and small groups of visitors awkwardly sit in the guest chairs around the room, smiling at me and then mentally escaping through the window, holding their own thoughts while staring out at the sky.

"Happy as a fluffy duck, I am," the boy says. "She's okay now, wasn't sure there for a minute," and the group nods, their eyes wide, as Ghost sings, her voice trying to break through and tell them that she isn't okay. But the boy just smiles, and the group nods, and I close my eyes and listen to her sing.

CHAPTER 36

My Voice Box

ONCE UPON A TIME, Ghost was in love with a boy. After the gods saved her life, she buried him deep inside us and promised she would never leave. But there is another story. Ghost has not hidden this one. It is where my voice box is. I remember everything, because I was there.

Inside the boy's house, in the living room, the television is playing. The sun is bright because it is summer, and the wind is playing with the curtains. Down the hall, in the kitchen, the boy faces the coffee pot, standing in the same spot where he takes his shots. His eyes are distant, his mind somewhere else. But I remember this, I tell Ghost. I remember.

Ghost paints the picture in her own way: the boy in the sun-soaked kitchen, in the house they shared, and me, the uninvited guest, with her back to the washroom.

"I'm sad," I tell the boy. Ghost claws my throat, rattles my voice so the words come out like a wail. Like her song. My body, her body, is still. But she fills my ears with grief because this is her boyfriend. This is her house. This is her life.

"I know you are, it's obvious," the boy mutters.

He is quiet. Ghost's sharpened teeth are gnawing my esophagus, her thin fingers squeezing my heart, because this isn't right, and I am a thief.

"I think I should move out," I say, breathless.

Ghost bites my throat. She is not singing, she is screeching. The boy says nothing. His eyes are still elsewhere, his body strong, leaning against the oven.

"I don't know what to do," the boy finally responds. His lips in a straight line.

Ghost screams. And her photograph fades.

But I remember what happens next. I remember gathering flattened cardboard boxes from the recycling bin outside the hardware store. Arms burning, stretching, as I carry them back to the boy's house.

"You don't have to leave," he says one night, when the stars are half-hidden by the clouds.

I remember packing each one of her artifacts until she disappears from all areas of the boy's house. Until it looks as though she has never been there.

"You don't have to leave," the boy repeats.

"I do," I tell him, while Ghost promises that she never will.

a Love Letter

MY COLLECTION OF SELF-HELP BOOKS promise that I can quiet my Ghost with forgiveness. The plump-lipped, silky-haired authors have flown over addiction and abuse with their iridescent light. They tell me I can soothe Ghost with meditation, connection, and self-acceptance.

Jude tells me that I need to sleep more. Mama tells me that I am perfect just as I am.

So I build a fortress of gratitude between myself and the world, and Ghost whines because she would rather be in someone else's bed, skin to skin, blanketed in their heat and the sticky sleepiness of gin and soda. She craves the boy and her foul-smelling cigarettes. She slips between memories of dark alleyways and of the white stucco house where Mama and John lived, where there was a little room beneath the staircase, half hidden but still part of the world. Ghost tells me that this room was small and dark, and she would lie there for hours, listening to the outside world, hiding beneath a yellow woollen blanket.

"This is my life," I whisper to Ghost, and in response she sings, grabs my hand, and swings me down dark lanes with the boy, her neck shadowed by his mouth, his thick leather belt, his wired grin.

"This is my life," I repeat, and I think of my smoky-eyed Jude; memories of them are now buried in my tibias, memories of the scent of sugar and of water lapping over my body, of how I feel at home both beneath the waves and in their bed. Of how I love warmth and pasta. The crunch of leaves. The view of the mountains. That feeling when the rest of the world is quiet. And Ghost's song.

The bus carries me home from Jude's house, over the border and back to my city with the big grey buildings and busy people. It is past dark when I call the boy to finish our story.

I let the phone ring five times and then leave a message asking him to call me back. I can hear the desperation in my voice. I can feel the ache in this heart. The boy must have been listening, because he calls back a few minutes later.

"Hello?" My voice sounds tiny.

"You called?"

"Yes, I just … I wanted to say …" I close my eyes and let Ghost's voice box connect with my own, allow her lips to layer over mine for a moment.

"I love you," Ghost whispers into the receiver.

"I miss you so much," his voice cracks. "I've been wanting to tell you for years now, and I'm not sure how to say this."

I've already shoved Ghost away again, removed her lips from my own. "I just wanted to let you know."

The boy's breath is searching. "After your surgery, things were different," he continues. "I knew I wasn't what you needed any-more. I loved you so much. Every cell in my body burned after the surgery 'cause I felt the coldness between us, you know? It happened immediately."

Ghost's bony fingers are cupping my heart as she sinks back into my bone marrow and the thickest parts of my muscles. She is hiding again, and her wails have calmed to a slight humming. Her fingers slip through my own, and she whispers her story of the hospital corridor, being wrapped in thick hospital blankets like a swollen caterpillar, stored in the small, dark room where I was set to grow.

"I'm getting married," I tell the boy.

"Yeah?" he says.

"Somewhere by the water," I say, remembering the summer months with Jude, our bodies glistening.

"As long as you're happy," he says. "Listen, I gotta go. It's late, and I'm up hellish early tomorrow."

"Oh yes, of course." I stumble out of the conversation and hang up, looking out the window for something to comfort me but only seeing myself.

Ghost's song is still muted, still subdued, floating strands of *remember me* in this body we both call a home. I tear off my blouse and pants and climb into bed, pull the thin comforter around my body, cocoon Ghost and myself because warmth is important to us, and fall asleep in the dark.

$\mathscr{L}$

That night, I dream of the sun and the small park by Jude's apartment. The roads are marbled in grey concrete and wavering heat. Ghost walks toward the park, her art bag swinging and clipping her hip as she dashes across the road and disappears into the chaos of the city.

ACKNOWLEDGMENTS

To each one of my friends who generously read, listened to, and supported me on my journey. To the brilliant Sirish, who set so many stones for me, I am forever grateful. Thank you to all of the Joshua trees and to each one of the stars for granting my wish. I am so grateful for all of the writers in my orbit who took the time to read over my manuscript and guide me further. As well, to all the writers whose inspiring stories made my heart need to try as well. To the Writers' Union of Canada and BIPOC Writers Connect. To Monique Gray Smith, who gave me the gentle push to finish this book. I am grateful for Barbara Pulling, who built the roadways of this book, and for each editor in my corner, especially Catharine Chen. To Jazmin Welch for designing such a gorgeous read. To Arsenal Pulp Press for publishing my words and to Brian Lam for holding my story gently and envisioning all this manuscript could be. To my agent, Laura Cameron, thank you for loving Ghost and for your enthusiasm and determination to get her story told. To everyone who reads this book, falls in love, and creates. And a special thank you to Jude, the boy, and my Ghost, as this story belongs to you.

Tara Sidhoo Fraser is a queer writer and

creator who lives on the unceded territories of the Musqueam, Squamish, and Tsleil-Waututh Nations (Vancouver, Canada). A woman of South Asian and Scottish ancestry, she is split between family histories. In 2016, she graduated from the University of Victoria and has since published her stories with *Autostraddle* and *Anathema*.

tarasidhoofraser.com